# Mystical TRAVELER

How to Advance to a Higher Level of Spirituality

## SYLVIA BROWNE

**HAY HOUSE, INC.**
Carlsbad, California • New York City
London • Sydney • Johannesburg
Vancouver • Hong Kong • New Delhi

*Published and distributed in the United States by:* Hay House, Inc.: www.hayhouse.com • *Published and distributed in Australia by:* Hay House Australia Pty. Ltd.: www.hayhouse.com.au • *Published and distributed in the United Kingdom by:* Hay House UK, Ltd.: www.hayhouse.co.uk • *Published and distributed in the Republic of South Africa by:* Hay House SA (Pty), Ltd.: www.hayhouse.co.za • *Distributed in Canada by:* Raincoast: www.raincoast.com • *Published in India by:* Hay House Publishers India: www.hayhouse.co.in

*Editorial supervision:* Jill Kramer • *Design:* Tricia Breidenthal

### Library of Congress Cataloging-in-Publication Data

Browne, Sylvia.
  Mystical traveler : how to advance to a higher level of spirituality / Sylvia Browne. -- 1st ed.
      p. cm.
  ISBN-13: 978-1-4019-1861-3 (hardcover) 1. Spiritualism. 2. Spirituality--Miscellanea. I. Title.
  BF1272.B8725 2008
  299'.93--dc22                                        2007047109

ISBN: 978-1-4019-1861-3

11  10  09  08    4  3  2  1
1st edition, September 2008

Printed in the United States of America

*To my friend
and kindred spirit
Linda Rossi*

# Contents

# Introduction

As I've said on television and at lectures so many times, regardless of how we view the often-chaotic world, there is a tremendous spiritual movement afoot. At one time it was underground, but every day I find that it's *above* ground and doing quite well. The reason it was hidden for so many years wasn't because of secrecy, but rather because the planet wasn't ready for it yet.

With the advantage of having been on *The Montel Williams Show* for 17 years and doing readings for more than five decades, I've seen an increase in the search for spirituality by human beings in general. As such, in this book I want to explain what I've noticed in great detail, including how we can all become the advanced spiritual entities known as "mystical travelers." Some ministers in my church, the Society of Novus Spiritus, are already aware of all of this because they were present when my spirit guide Francine relayed this information many years ago.

For those of you who aren't familiar with her, Francine is my primary spirit guide, and she's been with me since I was born. (I also have a secondary guide, Raheim, who came to me later on, and I'll talk more about him further on in this book.) I am not only clairvoyant, but also clairaudient, so I actually hear Francine. In addition, I'm a trance medium, so she uses my body to communicate from time to time. If you've read any of my other books, then you know that she's a great researcher who has ferreted out the truth on subjects great and seemingly small, time and time again.

So, thanks to this new awakening (a search for real spirituality and not just dogma), I feel that it's time to uncover and explain how we get to this higher level and all that it entails.

### *What Is Your Legacy?*

The fact that so many people are concerned about their spirituality comes with a twofold understanding: (1) There is definitely a time when Earth's reincarnation schematic is going to end, and (2) this planet will then cease to support life as we know it. (I feel that we have about 100 years left, possibly less.) Many individuals realize this in their souls and thus want to make the world a more holy place. They know that from the beginning of time, there has been a battle between good and evil, so they want to "step up to the plate" in some way. There is an unresolved feeling inside these men and women that makes them want to do more to raise their spirituality to a higher level. Their souls yearn to become something, but they don't know the name for it . . . they just have this feeling.

With all the stress we face on a day-to-day basis, including criticism about the way we sleep, exercise, become ill, wage war, fight terrorists, or deal with plagues and poverty, it's no wonder that many of us often feel like London during the "blitz" of World War II. We're constantly bombarded with news, and most of it is bad. We may even feel so defeated in a world that's ridiculously hectic and pulled in myriad directions—all seemingly headed nowhere—that we end up tired, impotent, and sick. We all seem to live with the "What if?" syndrome now, as we wait for misfortune to fall upon us.

The upside to this is that it's made many of us look for what's behind all the strife—and, even more important, what's *ahead* for all of us. Well, it's simple: We go to the Other Side with glory and a badge that says we did everything for our Creators. (The Other Side is our true Home, where we live when we're not incarnated on Earth, and I will talk much more about that concept throughout this book. In addition, our Creators consist of Father *and* Mother God. Please note that both of our "Parents" make up one God, so when I refer to God, I mean both of Them.)

It's all right to have your eye on who may be Mr. or Ms. Right, or even what car or house you're going to get, because our Parents don't deny ambition and comfort. It's only when they turn into the be-all and end-all of life that you'll find such aims some-what empty. The old saying "You can't take it with you" is so true; instead, ask yourself, "What *will* I take with me?" The answer should refer to your spirituality, your deeds, and how you've loved others . . . be it unconditionally or selfishly.

Yes, I'm talking about your legacy here—not the monetary or material kind, but how you've loved, treated, and done for others. Personally, I hate to go to funerals, but they're usually fine indica-tors of what men and women have done with their time on Earth. Unless they were celebrities of some sort, the number of people who file past the caskets or attend the burial ceremonies will point to how decent the individuals were and how many friends they had.

Naturally, we're all going to die someday. Yet since this planet is the harshest place in the universe, just to survive is an accom-plishment. But the key is *how* you survive: Do you just plod along in "survival mode" from day to day; or do you do good works, treat people with love and kindness, and finally go Home with dignity and your great spirituality intact? If you prefer the latter option, then that's where the mystical traveler comes in.

### Help Is All Around

The road you choose in life is called the "blueprint" or the "blue line," and it does run through hills and valleys. Even though you may feel that the particular road you're on gets washed out or overgrown with weeds, just keep moving straight ahead. If you do so, your angels will help you . . . and before long, a mystical traveler will show up.

In other words, when you feel that you're in a dead space—what I call "the desert period"—not only can you turn to Mother and Father God, your spirit guide, and angels; but you can also call on the mystical traveler, and he or she will absolutely help minimize your anguish. And know that even mystical travelers go through these periods, just like everyone else. (This also explains why these souls tend to encounter more adversity than others, but they also enjoy greater highs.)

Don't get into that hole of depression that has you feeling: *There is no one here who loves me* or *No one likes me; no one is here for me*. This is a pity party that spirals you downward, and you don't need that. Try to remember that you have all this protection walking beside you, not to mention your loved ones on the Other Side who also help you.

✠

Francine explains that Earth really is the toughest of all planets, and that those who come here often want to perfect their souls—and that's the reason why we have so many mystical travelers nowadays. She goes on to say that she is a mystical traveler herself and that there has never been an advanced entity who resented it or didn't want it.

Lots of people who never thought of becoming mystical travelers will in fact do so, my guide states, because they see how much spirituality is needed on this planet. When these souls constructed their Charts (the life plan individuals choose to help them learn and advance their souls) on the Other Side, they noted the world's insanity of war, pestilence, and humans' inhumanity to others and even animals—thus, they left open the option to become mystical travelers.

My spirit guide explains that even if someone were totally ignorant, he or she would still see, hear, or read about all the negative events that are happening every day across the globe. She says that those on her side are fully aware of what's going on here on Earth; and spirit guides, especially, talk about it among themselves. In fact, all on the Other Side are now convinced that it is the start of the end of days for this reincarnation schematic. I've said many times that in the last couple of decades I've seen more people who are on their last lives than ever before. And it's these individuals who tend to become mystical travelers.

Francine relates that there are more advanced entities here than on any other planet in existence, and more and more are coming in almost daily. She also claims that an amazing amount of babies being born now will be mystical travelers; however, most who become such souls actually ask to do so while already in life. This makes sense to me because if you're in a spiritual battle, you'd be smart to call for more troops *and* to make sure that your own armament was strong—not only for your own protection, but also to help the world come to spirituality before the last hurrah, so to speak.

If you're so inclined, you can become a mystical traveler yourself, but I must emphasize, *only if you can give it your all.* You see, becoming such an entity won't negate your chart; rather, you'll go through the same things you would have anyway, but you'll do so with greater aplomb. This may sound confusing at first, but once you understand what's happening, it all falls into place.

### Mystical Travelers and Mission-Life Entities

Along with the mystical traveler, there is another type of existence that entails great spirituality: that of the *mission-life entity.* It is more simplified, yet no less spiritual—in fact, most spiritual people are almost automatically mission-life entities. The mystical traveler is a higher form of the mission-life entity and is more complex and harder to achieve. These two groups are the only ones who have open options built into their charts while they're living, and all who decide to incarnate have the choice to become members of these two advanced groups.

As we know, everything in our life charts is written and chosen by us, but the only option left open in those charts is to become a mission-life entity or mystical traveler. This option entails a high level of spirituality and oneness with Mother and Father God that many choose not to have. You see, all incarnations taken on by white-souled entities are basically internal contracts made between us and our Parents for our own advancement of soul. (I will explain the difference between white and dark souls later in the book.) But lives taken on by mission-life entities or mystical travelers demand a greater and more substantial commitment to Them that goes beyond what we might say is our normal duty.

Nevertheless, it seems that in the last 20 years, people have become more and more conscious of this path . . . not that we haven't had those who experienced it all throughout history. For example, mystical travelers certainly lived in or around the time of Jesus, and many were part of the age of the Knights Templar. These days, such souls can be quite prominent, while others are basically unknown except to our Creators, which in essence is most important. In fact, you can be either a mystical traveler or a mission-life entity yet not give it a name, but I feel that naming things and providing directions to them gets us there faster.

### Pilgrims and Pioneers

All mystical travelers usually go down one of two paths: either that of the *pilgrim* or the *pioneer.* Pilgrims are the mystical travelers who are more quiet and work behind the scenes to help others. These are the hospice people, the individuals who adopt kids no one wants, and the men and women who tirelessly work as the caretakers of children and the elderly.

Pioneers, on the other hand, are more in the public eye and might even gain some fame as a by-product of their work. They're the ones who start spiritual movements, those teachers or writers who get the word out there.

It is within these two categories that mission-life entities come into play, since they often assist mystical travelers in their work. By dedicating their lives to helping mystical travelers succeed, they then perform their own missions. Now, please know that no one is better than another: How an individual wants to advance his or her spirituality for God is left up to that person. Realize that if we're mystical travelers, mission-life entities, or neither, our Parents love us all equally.

Rarely will a person go directly to mystical-traveler status without first being a mission-life entity. While this book is dedicated to the former, I'd like to thoroughly explain the latter. Mission-life entities are more common; in fact, anyone who consistently performs acts of kindness for others could fall under this category. And to a keen observer, the life themes (listed in the next chapter) of those who are predisposed to be on a mission for God are obvious just by sight.

Some souls are more advanced than others, and many of them aren't even consciously aware of being mission-life entities—even so, they did choose a mission to *accomplish* in life. Ben Franklin and George Washington were great mission-life entities, as is Billy Graham today. Almost all of the black people who were enslaved or the Jews who were put in concentration camps were mission-life entities, and many went on to become mystical travelers.

You may ask why mission-life entities tend to be so persecuted. Well, it's because they are reflections of this planet's inhumanity, such as the witch hunts, the so-called ethnic cleansings, the genocides, and numerous other atrocities. These souls choose their lives of pain in the hopes that humankind will notice and do things differently. This doesn't mean that all mission-life entities suffer, but they're definitely the white-souled individuals who love God and come in as sacrificial lambs. Through their sacrifices, they try to teach the world just what darkness, goodness, and courage really are.

I don't think that many on Earth have learned such lessons because we still have so much prejudice and bigotry—look at the plight of the Native Americans and other ethnic groups. I'm sure that you scream out at injustice just as I do. I'm really inclined to do so at my lectures, but even then I can feel as if I'm merely a marble in a giant drum or that I'm spitting into the wind. . . .

If you've never been persecuted, that doesn't mean you're disqualified from being a mission-life entity. These souls are the ones who are constantly auditing themselves, trying to determine whether or not they're on track, and many times they come in to take care of certain things, which doesn't necessarily mean that they must endure brutality or die as martyrs. For example, the doctor or researcher who comes up with the cure for a disease, the laypeople who start a group or foundation to help others or who bring to light a cause worth fighting for, or the leader or politician who sparks a government's corruption reform are examples in which a mission to accomplish or change something for the betterment of humankind is chosen.

Other examples of mission lives might be becoming a foster parent, founding a charity, or even beginning a business that employs others—that is, these existences can take many forms. When you get right down to it, almost everyone is on a mission of sorts, even if it's just to survive on this negative planet.

If you're a mission-life entity, you're given many gifts by our Creators, and even if you don't have the power of the mystical traveler, you can generally still hold your own against darkness. And it's absolutely true that if you choose to become such a soul, you will ascend the ladder to spirituality. It really is just what you want and what you feel better or more comfortable with. I can't say this enough: *Father and Mother God love everyone in the same way, and you don't have to be a mystical traveler to be an individual who greatly pleases Them.*

We all come in to life to learn and do the best we can, but it's up to us to make our lives really matter, both for our Parents and for our own advancement. In other words, *we're* the ones who want or need to gain a higher understanding in our souls—They don't ask us to do so.

✝

If you don't become a mystical traveler, this by no means should discourage you or make you feel inferior. When you decide to become more spiritual in general—whatever that means to your own God center—then you're on track. You always have the means to do so, even if it's just by asking and studying.

A lot of folks don't want a choice; they let others make their spiritual selections for them. You mustn't give up your soul's advancement by allowing anyone else to do this for you—even if it's to be a mystical traveler or mission-life entity. If you decide *not* to become either (although most white souls are mission-life entities, whether they know it or not), please keep in mind that Mother and Father God love us all equally and unconditionally. You must always "level up" for your *own* soul's spirituality, not to please Them. Make your own decision, and if it feels right, then it simply is.

It's also important to note that some people can be mystical travelers and not know it, while others can be *like* them. There are countless good men and women in this world doing great works, and not all of them have chosen to be mystical travelers. But for those who do so, it is powerful and eternal. Many mission-life entities do outstanding things in life, but they don't have the power and the movement or freedom that the mystical traveler does. Again, don't ever think that being on a mission life is any small feat: Most mission-life entities are actually very evolved and often align themselves with mystical travelers. There is power in the mission-life entities, and they will fill in and provide relief when mystical travelers are concerned with larger and more dangerous problems.

Francine does say that those who become mystical travelers become even whiter in their souls than ever before, but the whiter the entity, the more it must battle darkness (or, I should say, the more it is *aware of* darkness). She also warns that mystical travelers "cannot stand negativity, cannot bear harshness, cannot stand injustices, and cannot stand hypocrisy."

My spirit guide adds that mystical travelers don't just become happy-go-lucky blobs, filled with nothing but love, sweetness, and light. No, they are warriors of righteousness and temperament, as well as fiery and passionate whenever they are righting wrongs. Being a warrior doesn't necessarily mean going to war, but mystical travelers are steadfast in their beliefs and unshakable in their smiting of darkness.

Remember, even if you ultimately decide not to take on the mantle of mystical traveler, you can always call on those who *have* to help you. And if you realize that you would like to set out upon this path, the following chapters will explain the category further and even walk you through becoming such an advanced soul.

Ultimately, no matter what you decide, this book will help you improve your life!

✦ ✦ ✦

# CHAPTER ONE

# THE MAKEUP OF A MYSTICAL TRAVELER

The highest and most advanced spiritual level you can obtain in this life is that of mystical traveler. But fear not: It isn't outwardly manifested through flogging; long fasts; or other forms of punishment, such as penance, denial, self-sacrifice, and loneliness. Becoming a priest, nun, minister, cleric, or rabbi doesn't guarantee that you'll become a mystical traveler, and such a soul is not automatically a saint, as interpreted by Christian dogma. (It turns out that everyone who gets to heaven or the Other Side is a saint in one form or another.)

It's true that most of my ministers are aware of the mystical-traveler phenomenon, but not even all of *them* have taken on the mantle, and that's absolutely fine. Please don't feel that by reading this book, anything is mandatory. It's interesting because Francine says that taking the oath of the mystical traveler is really for the souls who feel there must be "more"—they sense some form of unrest, as if an alarm has gone off and propelled them to something greater, but they don't have a name for it. Of course those who don't choose to be mission-life entities or mystical travelers can still advance for God.

As I've said before, becoming a mystical traveler is not for the faint of heart . . . in fact, in the beginning it is very, very hard. This oath should not be taken lightly because it marks your soul for Father and Mother God, aligning you especially with Her—you more or less join Her army for good. Think of having Mother God as your Commander after you've accepted the mantle.

✝

Since so many don't opt to become mystical travelers, and even fewer were created by our Parents, you may wonder what it is that pulls souls to such a high level of spirituality. I believe that of those who become mystical travelers, most can point to being on their last lives as the driving force to do so.

There are several reasons for this. First, by the time an individual soul has incarnated for the last time, he or she has been shown the need for great spiritual advancement over and over again. Second, the final existence is the last opportunity to become a mystical traveler in a realm other than the Other Side. And third, by the time a soul is done incarnating, a great deal of wisdom has been accumulated. Part of that wisdom is the knowledge that our Creators love us all unconditionally and would never ask us to do any more than we've already decided to do, nor would They ever give us more than we can handle.

Even though they're on their last lives here on this planet, mystical travelers will at any time be asked to go elsewhere in the galaxy to right wrongs. According to Francine, other worlds don't have the illnesses, wars, and chaos that Earth does, so at least it's some consolation that those of us who *have* taken on the mantle won't have to reside on any planet that has the insanity that this one does.

In addition, mystical travelers become imbued with healing abilities, whether it's through words or the laying on of hands. Since they've given up their will to Mother and Father God, Their grace comes right through such individuals to whomever they wish to heal or help.

When you become a mystical traveler, it doesn't mean that you automatically become a psychic and/or a healer, but it will eventually happen. Whether you decide to hang out a shingle is up to you, but you'll definitely feel yourself becoming more infused with spiritual knowledge and thus able to write about your journey and help other people with what you've learned. You may not always be right, but you'll be right more often than you're wrong.

Keep in mind that even Jesus was criticized and called evil and a charlatan. Despite his being the Messiah, his detractors couldn't see this, or understand that his real mission was to free them from the bondage of this world and make them understand that life is temporary. Yet although they crucified him, he triumphed in the end.

The world can be fickle, and the love you receive one minute can turn to disdain the next. But you can overcome this by keeping constant, always remaining on course, and staying honest. If you've fallen, be up front, for people tend to forgive everything but deception. Above all, never put yourself smugly above and ahead of others—if you do, then you become full of pride and self-righteousness. Who are you to look down on anyone? Keep in mind that in some of your other incarnations, chances are you were probably just as bad as the person you're currently judging.

### *The Six Levels*

It is known that there are seven levels on the Other Side and that individuals choose their life charts to advance for God. But please understand that entities on the third level of the Other Side can be just as advanced as those on the sixth. These levels are more occupational in nature: If you'd like to work with animals, you'd go to the third level; if you'd rather be a researcher, you'd go to the fifth level; if you'd prefer to teach, you'd go to the sixth level, and so on. (For a detailed explanation of these levels on the Other Side, please see my book *Exploring the Levels of Creation*.)

Let me stop here and state that if all you did was live this life and go to any one of the seven levels on the Other Side, then you would have perfected for God with excellence. Those who leave the option of becoming a mystical traveler open in their charts simply have something in their souls that pushes them toward a higher level of spirituality. There's certainly nothing wrong with leading a normal existence, and you do raise your spirituality by doing so—but when you become a mystical traveler, you take on much more than normal. It's like saying that you'll be attending Harvard instead of your local junior college.

Just as there are levels on the Other Side, there are also levels that you'll go through as a mystical traveler. However, these are sequential and are more like stages. Here they are, in order:

1. The first level is the subconscious (or I should say, "super-conscious") knowledge that there is something in your soul that's crying out for your attention. It's telling you that you need to advance to a higher level of spirituality, but you don't necessarily know that you're being called to be a mystical traveler.

2. The second level is the recognition that you want to be a mystical traveler, even if you still don't have a specific label for it.

3. The third level is wrestling with the knowledge of what becoming such an advanced entity might entail; you may have received this knowledge by infusion.

4. The fourth level is taking on the mantle of the mystical traveler, which is done by totally surrendering to the will of God. Once you embark on this path, there is nothing that can make you turn back or deflect or negate it. As they say, "As it is written, so it will be." However, at this stage there is no validation—only acceptance of your gift and what it entails.

5. The fifth level is the activation of the gift of being a mystical traveler. This means that you'll do and go wherever God's will directs you. Remember that such status won't override your chart but will make it more elongated and intense. You must keep in

mind that even before you came in to life, you wrote in the opportunity to become a mystical traveler or mission-life entity.

6. The sixth and final level is "graduation"; that is, going Home and getting your next assignment. After you go through the orientation process on the Other Side, you go wherever and do whatever God wishes.

✝

As they go through the levels, all mystical travelers will have a gold star appear where their so-called third eye is. It's not a visible marking, but rather something recognizable to the soul.

There's nothing uniform about these entities: They're not just tall, short, or dark- or light-skinned people; and they can be of any race, religion, creed, sex, or even sexual preference. Yet while there's no discernment in physical makeup or background, you can spot them by how they live their lives as an example for others. Now, some have converged in the same parts of the world—it used to be the coastlines that drew them—but as more come in or awaken to a spiritual realization, they've begun to move all across the continents.

There's no special age requirement to become a mystical traveler either; for example, I didn't accept the mantle until I was 50. Yet I believe that such an individual's existence is almost set up for it. For example, like so many of you, I always tried to live a good life by teaching, helping people, taking responsibility, and loving God. As I touched on before, if you're only taking care of family and friends and trying to bring about harmony and truth even on a small scale, then you're on the level of a mystical traveler.

Francine says that you never hear of these advanced souls losing their minds or being prone to depression for very long . . . as long as their sensitivity to others doesn't get the best of them. To take the oath is certainly not easy, but it's always done through free-will choice.

Can mystical travelers falter? Of course they can. Take Jesus at Gethsemane, when he asked God to remove the pain and ordeals that he knew he'd have to endure. We're pretty sure that the answer was no because, being the ultimate mystical traveler, Christ replied to his Father, "Thy will be done."

Yet as they progress through life, mystical travelers receive all kinds of "bonuses"—such as protection, more insight, or the gift of prophecy and even healing—for being who they are and for sending out such positive energy, such as through "light columns." Of course mystical travelers are not the only ones who can do this, which is simply the practice of consciously planting sparkling light columns from the Holy Spirit by affirming the following: *Wherever I walk, I will step and plant a column of light that reflects the Holy Spirit and depletes all darkness and negativity.*

In the mornings, I leave these columns on stairs, on the street, in hotel rooms, in offices, and wherever else I go when I put the white light of the Holy Spirit around me.

### Spreading the Light

Francine says that as mystical travelers' souls progress through their lifetimes, they'll try to gather together similar entities who are presently here on Earth or are coming back from other travels. And mystical travelers seem to know instantly when others like them need help . . . it's like a spiritual SOS that goes out. These advanced individuals find each other in life, even if they don't know that that's what they're called. There is no secrecy, no special meeting place, and no occult ritual for mystical travelers—they simply go out in the world to spread light and help others.

Speaking of spreading light, anyone can do the meditation that follows, which I call "At One with the Universe," but if you've taken on the mantle of the mystical traveler, it will carry more power:

*Begin by sitting cross-legged and placing your hands, palms facing up, on your thighs. I want you to call on all the hosts of heaven: God the Father, Jesus Christ, and dearest Mother God (also known as Azna).*

*You are in a very quiet and dark field at night. You are not afraid, because the darkness around you creates a mantle. You are sitting there in the darkness, and you are wishing for, or aspiring to, enlightenment. In the far-off sky, directly within your third eye's vision, appears a dot of light, so tiny at first that you think it will disappear in the blink of an eye. It is almost as if someone has taken a pin and pierced a velvet garment. You blink, but it is still there.*

*Visualize this pinpoint of light, which is a bluish silver in color. You sit transfixed by it, gazing at it so intently that it almost makes your eyes tear. That small dot starts to become larger—in a heartbeat, this ray of silver blue light shoots from the darkness, pierces through the night sky, and presses warmly into your very being.*

*All of a sudden, you are aware that there are millions of tiny lights, like fireflies, which begin to dot the night sky. You feel that you are bombarded in the most wonderful way by these pinpoints of light hitting different parts of your being, like lasers that clean out darkness. All of these fireflies of light now seem to be dancing around you.*

*Way off in the distance, you hear the sound of the most unbelievable music—it is very soft at first, but it begins to roll toward you, like a wave coming in. You can almost feel the sound eating up the molecules of space as it moves toward you. Every fiber in your being is now alert, and adrenaline is pumping life-giving fluid to all parts of your body.*

*You know that you are synthesized with the universe—it is not only a part of you, but you are a part of it. And the universe is aware because you have addressed it . . . all the sensations, emotions, and beneficence are poured down from it to you. Over all of that stands God, watching from a distance. What is even more miraculous is that this Great Caretaker is watching from the present, watching from the past, and watching from the future.*

*You now have splinters of light that can shoot off your fingertips, and the light has also been imbued inside your body. You have been given healing ability, along with the rapture of being cemented with the light that came from, and was created by, God.*

*You stand in this field, and you are illuminated. You shine like a silvery knight: armored, protected, smiling, fervent, loyal, honorable, dedicated, constant, responsible; and with sword glistening. Feel your foreverness. Feel your continuation. Feel your power. In the name of Mother God, Father God, and Jesus, ask that they attend to you on this day for healing, comfort, and sanctity.*

*Bring yourself up, all the way up, feeling absolutely marvelous . . . imbued with knowledge, inspiration, and healing.*


### Life Themes and the Mystical Traveler

When you accept the mantle of the mystical traveler, you may see changes right away. But it will also take a good year for it to sink into your soul, as well as to rid yourself of old wounds and bad memories from all of your lives. In addition, you must make a concerted effort to keep giving up your will totally and unconditionally to God. The human part of you can have doubts about being able to do so, especially when you start asking yourself, "But what if God's will is against everything I want?" Well, I went through this, too, and it just isn't a valid concern. Your chart stays the same but becomes more intense, and your involvement with people and their needs becomes imperative in your life.

Now, when you become a mystical traveler, that role *can* override your life themes (which are detailed at the end of this chapter), so they may no longer have as much impact on your chart. For example, my themes are Humanitarian and Loner—yet when I took on the mantle, the Loner theme fell away, but the Humanitarian theme became more and more accelerated. I still am who I am with my chart intact, but being a mystical traveler accentuated everything. Remember that I didn't become one until I was 50 . . . and then all of a sudden, speaking engagements cropped up, I wrote my first book, and I began going on lecture tours to the tune of 30 or 40 a year.

However, I still followed my track: I remain a mother and grandmother, I live in the same place, and I have the same staff. I go shopping, take care of my dogs, eat with my friends, enjoy crafts, and so on. What I'm trying to show here is that I'm still Sylvia, but now I'm more the Sylvia who's on *Montel,* writing, giving lectures, and *doing.*

If you become a mystical traveler, do you have to start a church and preach unto the heavens? No, but you *will* be called on as a witness to our all-loving Creators and must bear that witness to the world. This is why I say that if you pay close attention, you'll be able to pick out mystical travelers. Such souls lead good lives as an example to all, in addition to doing many great works, so if you're aware enough, you can spot them in your everyday life.

There are several ministers in my church (the Society of Novus Spiritus), such as Loren and Virginia in my Seattle branch, who were mystical travelers before they ever heard of the moniker. One always recognizes another, so I definitely recognized John and Gloria Amman, as well as many other members of my Campbell, California, branch. Some took the oath and moved away, but they'll always carry it with them, no matter where they go. For example, one person went on to write a spiritual book, while another pursued a technological career and brought light to everyone. Now I'm not just talking about my ministers here, but rather some wonderful laypeople who once attended our church and went out in the world with their mantle and made it a better place.

⁜

Although taking on such a mantle requires that mystical travelers give up their will as part of their commitment to Mother and

Father God, that commitment can take on several different forms. It seems that almost all advanced entities have specialties or fields of endeavor that are close to what we'd describe as passions. One isn't greater than another; some mystical travelers take on more than one of these passions, and many specialties seem to intertwine with one another. However, for informational purposes, all mystical travelers generally fall into one or more of the following categories: Caretakers, Cause Fighters, Healers, Humanitarians, Prophets or Psychics, or Rescuers. All of these are noble pursuits and benefit humankind in one way or another.

These are the Mother Teresa types who rescue, care for, heal, and help those in dire need; if nothing else, they let people who are suffering die with dignity. These are the individuals who run hospices for children, the elderly, and the sick and dying. These are the men and women who start foundations or provide housing and care for the homeless. These are the healers—doctors, nurses, counselors, or even those who do the laying on of hands or holistic work. These are the individuals who foretell future events and give out information that's infused from God to help others make better decisions and live their best lives. These are also the folks who raise their voices against injustice, such as Dr. Martin Luther King, Jr., Abraham Lincoln, and the like.

All of these works are done every single day by inhabitants of our world, and they're all manifestations of God through Their creations. Out of the millions who have done (and do) these good deeds, you'll find mystical travelers interspersed within them. Some are easy to recognize, like those mentioned above, but most won't become famous, because that's not what they seek. If they do become well known, it's generally a direct effect of the huge impact they've made on so many lives.

Such advanced souls seem to come in to this life for a singular purpose, and that's to positively change the world. No matter how small that change may be, it still makes a difference. Let's say, for instance, that there are two parents whom the general public is unaware of, but they foster the spirituality to raise a mystical traveler. That in itself puts them on the level of being mystical travelers. Their names may not be in lights, but they go about their daily lives planting light columns of spirituality, often without knowing it—simply because they're good people.

Mystical travelers always end up being great teachers, oftentimes just by living exemplary lives. Along with many occupations that they might take on, these entities can also be leaders of people, but usually in what we call a quiet way. Their leadership tends to be more behind the scenes, most likely through spoken or written words. They're never self-aggrandizing or full of greed, avarice, or jealousy; but they do fight against the false prophets or authorities who dole out erroneous, harmful, or even silly or fantastic information to gather followers.

The mystical-traveler mantle really puts a fire in your belly, but along with that it seems that you gain endurance and joy. Yes, you can also be hurt by the lying skeptics who try to defame you, but the delight of your love affair with the world makes all the hateful naysayers go away. (I talk much more about dealing with skeptics in Chapter 8.)

It's interesting to note that each of the groups I mentioned a few pages back is also a life theme, but that doesn't necessarily make everyone who's taken on the themes of Caretaker, Cause Fighter, Healer, Humanitarian, Psychic, or Rescuer mystical travelers. However, I do feel that it's helpful to list all of the themes here. In this way, you can familiarize yourself with them, as well as more easily understand the type of person who would be attracted to becoming a mystical traveler. Again, I must stress that we're all equal in God's eyes, so no theme is better than any other.

(Please note that some of the themes relate to a type of person [such as Activator or Loner]; while others refer to a tendency, condition, or predilection [such as Aesthetic Pursuits or Intellectuality].)

## The 47 Life Themes of Humanity

**1. Activator.** The focus here is to perform tasks that others have failed to accomplish. These may be truly gargantuan or quite menial, but the focus is always on getting the job done right. Activators, often called activists, are the turnaround artists or the troubleshooters of the world—the ones who successfully reverse failure. Naturally, these entities are in great demand and so have a tendency to spread themselves too thin. Activators should make every effort to confine their energies to tasks where a genuine opportunity to achieve beneficial change exists.

**2. Aesthetic Pursuits.** Music, drama, painting, sculpting, and writing are included in this category. An aesthetic theme is not to be confused with a little "flair" for one of those enterprises; rather, when an aesthetic theme is present, the entity is driven by his or her innate talent. A need to create manifests itself at a young age and dominates the individual's entire life.

**3. Analyzer.** The rest of us learn from the Analyzers' continuing scrutiny of the most minute details, for they want to know everything about a subject, including how it works and why. Analyzers are afraid that they'll miss something or that some detail will be overlooked, so they thrive in scientific or highly technical settings where their skills are vital. In everyday situations, their challenge is to let go and trust the senses. After a discreet analysis of the behavior of others, Analyzers should ask the Holy Spirit for enlightenment to transcend the physical evidence.

**4. Banner Carrier.** The first lieutenant of the **Cause Fighter** may be found picketing, demonstrating, or lobbying; these entities also fight the battle against injustice. The keys to success in perfecting this theme are moderation, tact, and discrimination—it's far better for these entities to select one cause and see it through than to scatter their impact among many.

**5. Builder.** These entities are the cornerstones of society, the unsung heroes and heroines of wars, home life, and organizations. Good parents are often Builders, enabling their children to paint on a much larger canvas. Without these cogs, the wheels of society would never turn, yet Builders rarely receive credit for the accomplishments made possible by their efforts. They need to keep in mind that not all prizes are won on this plane of existence—often those who get the credit on Earth are not actually perfecting as rapidly as Builders are, who help make their accomplishments possible.

**6. Caretaker.** As their name implies, these entities take care of people, and generally do so happily. (Rosie, my childhood maid, looked after our house, walked me to school when I was little, and spent her whole life joyously being a part of our family until she died. She'd been married at one point, but her husband had died in World War II. She then became attached to my grandmother, and thus came to care for all of us in the family.)

**7. Catalyst.** Here are the networkers and innovators, those agents of change who make things happen. Catalysts are the classroom stars whom everyone aspires to be, the ones invited to parties to ensure excitement. Catalysts are essential to society for their innovations (Ralph Nader is a prime example), generally have boundless energy, and actually appear to thrive on stress. They must have an arena in which to perform, however, or they become morose and counterproductive.

**8. Cause Fighter.** The number of crusades is infinite—peace, whales, hunger, and so on—and the Cause Fighter will either be drawn to them or will create more. These entities fulfill an important function by speaking for others who are perhaps too absorbed with their own themes to address social issues. Cause Fighters have a tendency to be impulsive that can place themselves and others in jeopardy, so it's essential that they consider the possibility that the cause itself may be minimal compared to their ego involvement.

**9. Controller.** The challenge for this entity is obvious; in fact, Napoleon and Hitler were typical examples of this theme manifested in its most negative sense. Controllers feel compelled to not only run the overall show, but to dictate to others how they must perform the smallest details of their lives. In order to perfect, these entities must learn self-control and restraint.

**10. Emotionality.** Both euphoric highs and devastating lows—and every subtle nuance of emotion in between—will be felt by entities with this theme. Emotionality is often a characteristic of poets and artists, and it will indeed enhance creativity while imposing a severe challenge. The recognition of a need for balance is vital here, as is the establishment of intellectual self-control.

**11. Experiencer.** It's not unusual for this entity to go from flower child to bank president to vagabond touring the world in a self-made boat. Experiencers dabble in nearly everything and master many of their pursuits, and wealth is merely a by-product of their multifaceted endeavor (Howard Hughes is a well-known example). Good health is essential to Experiencers, so it's important that they don't jeopardize it with excesses.

**12. Fallibility.** Entities with this theme appear to always be at the wrong place at the wrong time, for they've entered life with a physical, mental, or emotional handicap. Helen Keller, who as an infant contracted a fever that left her deaf and blind, is an excellent example—her triumph over these so-called hindrances is an inspiration to everyone. It's important for entities with a Fallibility theme to remember that they chose this path in order to set an example for the rest of us.

**13. Follower.** Initially, these entities might have preferred to be **Leaders**, but on some level they decided not to make the necessary commitment. The challenge of the Follower is to realize that leadership is impossible without them and thus recognize their own importance. Perfection comes from accepting their self-chosen theme and providing the Leader with the best support possible. Yet discrimination is also necessary here in deciding exactly who and what to follow.

**14. Harmony.** Balance remains vitally important to entities with this theme, and they'll go to any length to maintain it. Their personal sacrifices are admirable up to a point, but the real challenge lies in the acceptance of life's wrinkles. Remember that what can't be changed must be adapted to and accepted.

**15. Healer.** These entities are naturally drawn to some aspect of the healing professions, be it physical or mental. The good they do is obvious, and the only danger is that they can easily become too empathetic. It's imperative that those with a Healer theme pace themselves so that they avoid burnout.

**16. Humanitarian.** While **Cause Fighters** and **Banner Carriers** cry out against the wrongs committed against humankind, the Humanitarian theme takes these entities into the action itself. Humanitarians are too busy bandaging, teaching, holding, and saving to have time for protests. Those in this category aren't all that concerned with the concept of evil, and they're inclined to excuse humankind for its faults. Humanitarians rarely *just* help their family and friends, but tend to reach far beyond to anyone who touches them. As a result, they're in danger of overextending themselves. The challenge for the Humanitarian—*my* challenge—is to avoid physical burnout through self-love and nourishment.

**17. Infallibility.** Entities in this category are born rich, attractive, witty, and so forth. Yet when we consider that perfection is everyone's universal goal, we find that this theme is actually one of the most challenging. There's often a tendency toward excesses of all kinds here, almost as if the entity wants to tempt fate. Curiously, there may often be a lack of self-esteem that causes those with the Infallibility theme to fear that they aren't lovable as individuals. The goal here is to truly accept the theme and learn to live with it.

**18. Intellectuality.** Here is the theme of the professional student. Charles Darwin—who used the knowledge that he acquired through intensive study to experiment, hypothesize, and eventually publish—is an excellent example of one who has perfected this theme. But since knowledge for its own sake is frequently the goal among intellectuals, there's often a danger that the knowledge they've so ardently sought and painfully acquired will go nowhere.

**19. Irritant.** Deliberate faultfinders, entities with this theme are essential to the perfection of others, for in their company those around them are forced to learn patience and tolerance. Although it's important not to buy in to the Irritant's innate pessimism, those in their orbit must also be nonjudgmental and remember that Irritants are perfecting their themes so that others can perfect theirs through *them*.

**20. Justice.** Many of America's Founding Fathers, concerned as they were with fairness and equality, are examples of the Justice theme in operation, as are those who eagerly help out and provide the authorities with information when they've witnessed an accident or crime. As admirable as all this sounds, it's imperative that these entities use discretion in their choices and remain God centered.

**21. Lawfulness.** Practicing or teaching law is an obvious choice for these entities, who are almost obsessed with issues of legality, while others in this category may be found serving on governing boards. When elevated, these souls keep the world safe and balanced, but they must always be on guard against the possibility of using their power in a self-serving manner.

**22. Leader.** Those who possess this theme are self-controlled, premeditated, and rarely innovative, choosing to take charge in areas that are already established. Their drive is toward success rather than creation, and their challenge is to avoid "power trips."

**23. Loner.** Although often in the vanguard of society, those with this theme invariably pick occupations or situations in which they're isolated in some way. (This is a secondary theme of mine, for being a psychic has set me apart from others.) Loners are generally happy with themselves but should watch their irritation levels when people come into their space. If each theme recognizes the presence and significance of other themes, the result will be far greater tolerance and understanding in the world, and—eventually—peace.

**24. Loser.** These entities are extremely negative, although unlike those with the **Fallibility** theme, they're born without handicaps. Often Losers have many good points, but they choose to ignore them. Although their theme may resemble that of the **Irritant**, with their proclivity for constant criticism, they're different in that they invariably place the blame back on "poor me." These entities are prime martyrs, moving from one elaborate soap opera to another. It's important that we not judge the people who have this theme, remembering that their patterns were chosen to enable us to perfect ourselves—and by observing them in action, we'll endeavor to be more positive.

**25. Manipulator.** This is one of the most powerful themes, for Manipulators are easily able to control situations as well as people. By viewing life as a chessboard, those with this theme can move individuals and circumstances to their advantage, as though they were pawns. (President Franklin D. Roosevelt was a prime example of a Manipulator in action.) When such a person works for the good of others, this theme is elevated to its highest purpose. However, when the theme is misused, the ultimate goal of perfection takes a long time to achieve.

**26. Passivity.** Surprisingly, entities with a Passivity theme are actually active—but about nothing. Although they'll take stands on issues at times, it's always in a nonviolent manner. Of course, any extreme is hurtful to the individual, but *some* tension may be needed in order to bring about the perfection of the soul.

**27. Patience.** The Patience theme is clearly one of the most difficult paths to perfection, as those with it seem to desire a more rapid attainment than entities with less challenging themes. Often, they carry great amounts of guilt when they feel that they've strayed from their goal, resulting in their impatience. This attitude can lead to self-abasement and suppressed anger. These entities must be lenient with themselves, for it's difficult enough living through the circumstances that they've chosen in order to express this theme.

**28. Pawn.** Whether the means are negative or positive, Pawns trigger something of great magnitude into being (the biblical Judas is a classic example of this theme). We can't evolve toward universal perfection without the Pawn, but those entities who select this theme should preserve their dignity by only picking worthy causes.

**29. Peacemaker.** These entities are not as tranquil as the name implies. Peacemakers are actually pushy in their desire for and pursuit of peace—they work endlessly to stop violence and war, addressing a larger audience than those who've opted for **Harmony** as a theme. And their goal of peace far exceeds an allegiance to one particular group or country.

**30. Perfectionist.** We should all want things clean and orderly in our lives, yet entities with this theme can go that extra step and be very innovative at work, thus saving time and money. Perfectionists also tend to be harder on themselves than anyone else. They demand that they do everything just right, with no opening for sloppiness. They believe that if you're going to do something, then you should do it right. If it gets to the point that it becomes an obsessive or compulsive problem, then this theme has to be tempered. Perfectionists may have to force themselves to leave their work or responsibilities and kick back for a time to recoup their energy.

**31. Performance.** Those with a Performance theme find it highly rewarding but frequently exhausting. These entities are the true "party animals"—some will go into actual entertainment careers, but others will simply be content to entertain in their homes or offices. The challenge here is for those with this theme to combat burnout by looking within, thus acquiring the ability to nourish and entertain *themselves*.

**32. Persecution.** Entities with this theme go through life in anticipation of the worst, certain that they're being singled out for persecution. Experiencing pleasure can throw them into a panic because they're convinced that somehow they must pay for it. This arduous theme is chosen to allow others to grow spiritually.

**33. Persecutor.** Those with a Persecutor theme may range from wife beaters and child abusers to mass murderers. It's difficult to see the purpose of this theme within a single life span, but these seemingly "bad seeds" have a self-chosen role to play that enables humankind to evolve toward perfection. Once again, it's imperative that we don't judge these individuals.

**34. Poverty.** The theme of Poverty appears most frequently in developing nations, yet it can be even more of a challenge in affluent societies. Some entities with Poverty as a theme may actually have all they need to be comfortable yet *feel* poor. With progress, the frenzy fades and is slowly replaced by a sense of bliss, as the realization comes that the trappings of this world are transitory things whose importance will quickly pass.

**35. Psychic.** The theme of Psychic is more a challenge than a gift, at least in the early stages. Entities with this theme often come from strict backgrounds where authority figures strive to deny or suppress their gifts of being able to hear, see, or sense things in a manner beyond that of "normal" perception. Eventually, these entities will learn to accept and live with their abilities, using them for good in a spiritual, if not professional, manner.

**36. Rejection.** This challenging theme manifests itself early, accelerating with the entry into school and subsequent involvement in relationships. Often these entities are deserted by those they love—even their own children will adopt surrogate mother or father figures. The pattern can be broken once the entity recognizes what's happening and surrenders the action and ego involvement to God.

**37. Rescuer.** One often finds the Rescuer working alongside the **Cause Fighter**, but when the Cause Fighter moves on to another crusade, the Rescuer remains to care for the injured party. An entity with a Rescuer theme has a high degree of empathy and can manifest strength for those in need. Even when people have obviously created their own problems, the Rescuer is determined to "save" them. By doing so, the Rescuer is often the one left hurt. This theme presents a tough road to travel, but the spiritual rewards are great indeed.

**38. Responsibility.** Individuals who have chosen the Responsibility theme embrace it with fervor rather than obligation, and they feel guilty if they don't take care of everyone who comes into their orbit. The challenge is to decide what is immediate and necessary and then to stand back and allow others to share in the assumption of responsibilities.

**39. Spirituality.** The quest to find a spiritual center is an all-encompassing one for entities in this category. (We find it in people such as Billy Graham and Mother Teresa, along with laypeople who give their lives, money, or time to contribute to humankind.) When the full potential of this theme has been reached, these entities become far-sighted, compassionate, and magnanimous; but while still involved in the search, they must guard against being narrow and judgmental in their views.

**40. Survival.** For any number of reasons, real or imagined, life is a constant struggle for those who've selected a Survival theme. At their best in a crisis situation, these souls take a grim view of day-to-day existence. The obvious challenge here is to lighten up.

**41. Temperance.** The challenge here is to avoid extremes, as entities with a Temperance theme are more than likely dealing with an addiction of one kind or another. Or they may have conquered the actual addiction but are still dealing with a residue of feelings about it. The key to combating the fanaticism that often characterizes this theme is moderation . . . the true meaning of temperance.

**42. Tolerance.** Entities choosing this theme must be tolerant about everything—world affairs, relatives, children, politics, and so forth. Their burden is so great that they'll often only choose one area to tolerate, remaining very narrow-minded about all the rest. But by recognizing their theme, these entities can meet the challenge and grow more magnanimous in the process.

**43. Victim.** These entities have chosen to be martyrs and sacrificial lambs. And through their example—dramatically displayed by the media—we're made aware of injustice. (President John F. Kennedy is one who pursued a Victim theme through his means of exiting the planet, his back pain, his family name, and the pressures placed upon him by his parents.) After having played their parts, many Victims may choose to rewrite future scripts by altering their masochistic tendencies.

**44. Victimizer.** People's Temple leader Jim Jones was a prime example of this theme in action—it's obvious that many lives, as well as many themes, interacted with his. In the tapestry of life, Jones's unique role may have been to focus public attention on cult abuse.

**45. Warrior.** These entities are fearless risk takers who assume a variety of physical challenges, so many go into some form of military service or law enforcement. Although it's important to temper aggression, it still remains that without Warriors, we would be prey to tyrants.

**46. Wealth.** This theme sounds like a great choice, but it's invariably more like a burden that leads to destructive behaviors if unchecked. As with any theme, its goal is to overcome its negative aspects. Wealth is a seductive tempter that acts like an addiction—it's very difficult to gain control of this theme, so it tends to become one's master. People with this theme may be obsessed with acquiring, growing, and hoarding money, unconcerned with the methods of acquisition or the consequences of their actions in their quest for more. Moral values are of no importance to those in this category, so it can take many lives to overcome due to its powerful effect on a person. When people do finally master Wealth, you find them freely giving away their belongings, with no desire for anything in return.

**47. Winner.** Unlike those entities with the theme of **Infallibility,** to whom everything comes easily, Winners strive to win with great tenacity, often gambling or entering contests. Perennial optimists, they're always certain that the next deal, job, or marriage will be the best. No sooner has one deal fallen through than they pick themselves up and go on to what they know will be a winning situation. President Dwight D. Eisenhower was a positive example of this theme. As a general, his unfailing optimism was inspiring; as President, his confidence had a calming effect. The challenge for these entities, which Eisenhower appears to have met, is to take a realistic approach to winning.

✦ ✦ ✦

# CHAPTER TWO

# THE CALL THAT RESONATES IN THE SOUL

We humans carry our parents' DNA, so a part of them lives within us, but of course our actual mothers and fathers reside outside of us and guide and guard us. So it is with our Divine Parents: There is an individual part of Them inside us all that propels us to our Divine purpose. Yet the main portion of Them lies *outside* of us.

Our genes and individual makeup constantly connect us to the Divine, whether we become mystical travelers or not, and this is what makes every single one of us unique and different. We all have our own covenants with Mother and Father God, which are never broken, no matter what we do. Our Creators don't love mystical travelers more; such individuals just seem to have stronger covenants with Them. Because advanced entities carry so much more responsibility than most, they have more of a temptation to fall, but their need to spiritually advance kicks and picks at them until they strengthen their will before finally surrendering.

Again, there is no shame or lack of responsibility in deciding not to become a mystical traveler; if you don't want to become one, you can still go on and fulfill your chart for the glory of God. It would be akin to not wanting to join the armed forces but still doing things to show your support at home. During World War II, for instance, many people sold war bonds, others made planes or parachutes, and still others gathered old metal and rubber for recycling—all efforts were necessary for supporting the cause and ultimately ensuring victory.

If you *have* written it into your chart to become a mystical traveler, you'll be told that you have the choice to do so either before or during this life. You may wait to do so or even put it off, but the desire to elevate your spirituality will keep pushing, to the point that it almost pummels your soul. You can certainly deny the calling, but it won't let you go. The mantle will begin to descend until you, with all your freewill choice, finally decide to accept it. It's almost like being knighted.

In fact, taking the oath of the mystical traveler reminds me of the Knights Templar, who tried to save the truth about Christ living beyond the Crucifixion, including his marriage to Mary Magdalene. They gave themselves over to guarding that secret with such ardor that they were tortured, burned at the stake, and almost wiped off the face of the earth . . . yet they still didn't reveal what they knew. Being a mystical traveler requires similar dedication, but it also asks that you have a tangible belief system and act on a philosophy of love, beauty, and truth that will create an extraordinary expansion of your soul.

The mantle can hover above you for lifetimes—until your acceptance of giving up your will for God comes into full force—and then it will drop. And once it does, it will never come off. I know that you may be hesitant about giving up your will, but please keep in mind that the only free will there is exists on the Other Side. When you become a mystical traveler, you'll thoroughly understand that your will is God's will, that your chart expands, and that you'll be called on to go anywhere and help anyone. You may say that this sounds like too much, but with this advanced-soul status comes a bonus of energy and the feeling of righteousness and purpose. Yes, you will be tested more, but you'll also be given extra strength to help you.

As Francine explains, "Once you accept the mantle of the mystical traveler, you also accept that you have a line directly to, with, and for God; and you will literally do Their bidding even above your own chart. Now, you may say that you have no more freewill choice . . . well, you didn't anyway, not in life. It's on the Other Side, when you choose and write your chart, that you have free will. In giving your will to God, you've just "leveled up" in your spirituality and evolvement of your soul. Your will is not in opposition to anything, and your actions just become more exaggerated insofar as you're going to selflessly teach, preach, help, study, research, and learn—all under the guidance and the bidding of God."

### *Heeding the Resounding Call*

Francine shares that when the call to become a mystical traveler goes out, it resounds throughout you. You'll know when you get the calling by the nagging sensation of *There must be something more;* however, that feeling is also courtesy of your spirit guide nudging you, reminding you that even before you incarnated, you were told by the Council (a group of highly evolved beings that helps you with your chart) that you were mystical-traveler material. It's much like what so many nuns and priests I've known have told me: It was as if something inside of them awakened, and they just knew that the lifestyle they'd chosen was *absolutely* for them. It is the call, my guide notes, that resonates in the soul. And you don't have to dress or speak differently . . . it's a very quiet oath between you and God.

Francine said that I didn't have the mantle drop until I started my church, and that I wrestled with it for at least five years before that. Why so long? Because I knew the awesome responsibility and sacrifices that would be involved. Of course I was also aware of the benefits, but I *am* human—I was afraid that I wouldn't live up to being a mystical traveler, that I couldn't totally give up my will and be in complete service to Mother and Father God.

Also, when I first took on the mantle (not so much now), it brought tremendous loneliness and isolation with it. It was like seeing a light that not many people could see—and only a few seemed to comprehend what I felt in the very depths of my soul. I didn't understand, as I do now, that when you take on this mantle, it guides *you* rather than *you* guiding it. So it took me until I was 50 years old to take the plunge. Yet I've been a mystical traveler now for 21 years, and that has made a big difference. I've watched the world turn toward spirituality and ask for more and more knowledge, and that's why I keep writing as fast as I can, to give out solace, as well as this information that I've received . . . before I leave this planet.

‡

Even though as a mystical traveler you give up your will, our Creators never call on you to do more than They know you can do. The reward of doing what They want, along with the subsequent overpowering rise in spirituality and grace, is indescribable at times. Your relationship with Them just becomes so much closer and more intimate that it seems to fill your soul with Their love to the point of wanting to burst. I can think of no greater reward here on Earth or the Other Side. In fact, I feel that to elevate oneself to higher spirituality is a *giant* plus in and of itself, but there are many other bonuses to being a mystical traveler.

First of all, these advanced souls don't have to adhere to any rules. Now, I don't mean that they can do anything they choose because that would defeat the purpose. Rather, being there for our Parents and going on missions for Them are the only things that govern them. In addition, these entities can ask other mystical travelers to go on missions with them. I'm sure that's why so many of my ministers and those in my study groups, as well as others who want people to know what loving Parents we have, signed on to be a force that would help eliminate guilt and fear. Like Jesus before them, these blessed men and women disseminate the truth about what our Creators are really like, and they try to prove to humankind what our Lord actually came here for—which wasn't to die for our sins.

Francine says that she's never seen as many mystical travelers in life as there are today. She has also noticed that almost every entity who incarnates now wants a greater degree of spirituality, which she attributes to the rising number of these advanced entities.

There is no limit to the number of mystical travelers, as anyone who isn't a dark entity and sincerely wants to advance his or her spirituality is welcomed. Mystical travelers will experience more than others in both positive and negative encounters; after all, how can you help someone if you haven't been in the trenches, too? The one saving grace is that they seem to bounce back and recuperate more easily from any and all adversity. This is yet another benefit of giving up their will and being example entities for God.

### A Lifetime Process

Now I'd like to introduce you to Raheim, the spirit guide I first became aware of around 1970. Like Francine, Raheim comes to me when I'm in trance, and he's an expert in so many things, including medicine, history, religion, and natural magic (which is his forte). In no way is he smarter than Francine; he just approaches everything from a more linear position because he's male. I thought that we'd benefit from his viewpoint on the subject of mystical travelers.

Raheim says, "Once you accept what you are or have taken on—that being a mystical traveler has its hardships—it becomes a wondrous, continual spiritual life forever. Of course, everyone is spiritual in one way or another; mystical travelers have just given up the overpowering need for things that are material and seem so important.

"That doesn't mean you'll be unable to live by the fruits of your labor, but materialism doesn't become your God. Mystical travelers become what we know as the spiritual pilgrims or messengers. While they are advanced spiritual entities, remember that their spirituality is without ego or a fake, faltering humility. They must live life with honesty, true humility, and gratitude in order to be privy to the gifts that are bestowed upon them."

Raheim goes on to state, "For any spiritual movement to take hold, it takes many years. Even though you give up your will and go through the mystical-traveler process, you can't expect results overnight. You may have broken through many old phobias and habits, but no matter how good you are, you're still coming out of a lot of darkness and negativity, which also contributes to the time it will take to be successful."

This isn't meant to imply that *you* are dark and negative; rather, everyone absorbs negativity just by living on this planet, and it takes time to get rid of it . . . sometimes as much as 20 years. Please don't become frantic when you read these words, for you may make it in a shorter period of time. However, it does usually take about 20 years.

As Divine as Jesus was, even he didn't start his vocation as a mystical traveler until he was 30. Before his public life and ministry, he went through a long incubation period to cleanse himself of the negativity that he'd absorbed in his life. Interestingly enough, Francine says that it's very common to become an advanced entity around the age of 30, which is also the age most of us return to when we get to the Other Side.

You may protest that you just started the process and don't think you have that many years left. Well, if you really don't have very long, then your time will naturally be shortened; as far as your just getting started goes, that's actually not true. If you look back over your life, I bet you'll find that you started on a spiritual path many years ago. You may have begun it in childhood, in young adulthood, or sometime later, but like most people on a spiritual quest, I'm sure you've spent several years on it.

Regardless of what (if any) religion you grew up with, the moment you started searching for answers was the beginning of your quest. Your questions, your research, your education, and your life experiences have all contributed to your spirituality. This is the "spiritual you," and it's probably not as undeveloped as you think. Becoming a mystical traveler is merely the *culmination* of your spirituality; and from the moment you take that oath, you use it to do good and help others.

If you review your past, you'll find the beginning of the spiritual you. Perhaps you said something to the effect of "I can't buy what those in authority are telling me. I have to do what I want, and I must have my own God in my own personal reality. I'm not even going to listen to what these people say about sin, damnation, or hellfire." That's when your spirituality started! It probably blossomed right away, but then you may not have seen it bear fruit for a long time. As that's just another step in the levels of the soul, you can either accept it or keep doing what you've been doing. After all, if you're living a good life and that's fine with you, then it's certainly fine with God.

But consider this: *Anything* you do or experience takes time. For example, while getting over a loved one's death never really ends, after three to four years the raw edge of it does diminish. Does that mean you can't conjure up the pain at any time? Of course you can! My father's passing, for instance, was more than ten years ago, but it's still painful even now. No, it's not the razor's edge it once was, although whenever I hear "Over the Rainbow," I'm reduced to tears because it was his song for me.

I know that if you're experiencing extreme anguish, you feel that it will never end, but I assure you it will. If it didn't, you couldn't live. Being on a higher spiritual plane, or aspiring to be, does help and fills your soul with love.

Keep in mind that most of life is about overcoming something. Being abused doesn't scar the soul by itself, for instance. When people carry such an experience with them for too long, they can't seem to drop it, so they let it flavor their whole existence. This is where being a mystical traveler can really be an asset because it diminishes time and softens the pain of illness, divorce, trauma, and the like.

Four- or five-year periods constantly repeat themselves in human life, such as in the length of time it takes for those who are introverted doormats to become more extroverted and stand up for themselves. It can also take this long if you're trying to meet Mr. or Ms. Right. I'm not saying that you have to wait that long to marry if you're currently with the person of your dreams—just be careful about running to the altar with someone you've just met. It can work, but only if you're truly in love, not lust.

Even when we get a job we love and have trained for, it takes time to feel secure and understand all the ins and outs of our chosen profession. Or look at child rearing and the worry that goes with it . . . which actually never ends. Oh, we may get a respite, but for us parents, we will be concerned about our children until the day we die.

The time of getting to the full realization of yourself and who you are, which is linked to spirituality, also takes at least four years. This is part of how long it takes to become a mystical traveler. If the time is lessened, it often has to do with your dedication.

As Raheim explains, "What this comes down to is that you shouldn't expect things to happen quickly in this harsh school of life. It takes time to get to a point where you're ready to put what you've been taught into play, as well as to get your own infusion from God. Infusion can be different for all mystical travelers—we are all individuals and have our personal makeup, so it's good that we approach with our own tools and use them in our own way.

"You can get information that accentuates your individual training, and when you combine that with your experience, you can sometimes shorten the time it takes to be a mystical traveler. But again, I must emphasize patience, for it will take some time. The only danger you can get into is feeling that you're smarter or more advanced than other mystical travelers. When you teach others to be such entities, which you will, you must drive that point home. If they don't get it, then situations will arise, always brought on by their own egos, in which they'll be rendered impotent."

Just as a reference point, Raheim has shared the names of some of the world's more noted mystical travelers. The list doesn't name those advanced souls who are currently living (except for the Dalai Lama, who is a fairly obvious choice), but does include the following: Jesus Christ, Buddha, Mohammed, the Báb, Mother Teresa, Joan of Arc, William Shakespeare, Thomas Edison, Albert Einstein, Madame Curie, Abraham Lincoln, Queen Victoria, and too many more to mention.

As you can see, not all mystical travelers are noted disciples, such as Mary Magdalene, Joseph of Arimathea, or Pope John XXIII (all of whom were in fact mystical travelers). They also come from the worlds of science, education, entertainment, politics, medicine, and on and on it goes. They can be firefighters, butchers, bakers, salespeople, mechanics, ditchdiggers, construction workers, or from any other walk of life. They may not have their names in lights, but they're still doing good works and helping people—such souls are just as great as those who become well known. The only reason I shared the prominent ones above was because those individuals had human flaws yet still did something to make the world a better place. Whether it was in a big or small way, it was all great to God, because such acts worked to light other candles across the globe.

Some might not even care about, or be aware of, giving up their will, instead likening themselves to being troubleshooters for God. Chances are that if you'd walked up to Mother Teresa and asked her what it was like to be a mystical traveler, she would have had no idea what you were talking about. Many advanced entities don't have the terminology . . . only the calling.

In 1991, Francine and Raheim both said there were only about 2,500 mystical travelers on Earth. Now they number in the millions, even if these souls don't know it. You might ask, "What's so important about advanced beings knowing that that's what they indeed are?" Knowing who they are increases their strength, and they're also privy to the many tools that are available to them. They may come upon those tools if they don't know that they're mystical travelers, but they won't fully understand how to use them.

Who knows what mystical travelers might do after they answer the call in their soul and accept their mantle? They could foster and give to the world another mystical traveler who builds on the family and becomes great. Or they might pull themselves out of the gutter or ghetto to help others. Or they may get AIDS but make life better for those who are similarly afflicted. Many times, these are the unsung heroes of the world, but they are shining in the light of God's eyes.

### Unconditional Love

As a mystical traveler, you're endowed with a great deal of psychic discernment and unconditional love. Such love always seems to pay back, but it may not be in the way you think. Unconditional love means that you purely cherish others' souls—but you never love evil, and you don't have to be at anyone's beck and call. That's where some Christian concepts such as "Love your enemy" go astray. I know that Jesus purportedly said to do this, but did he intend it to be taken literally, or did he mean to love the enemy's soul within? To take this to its most drastic point, let's think about those who are involved in war.

It would be illogical to say that everyone who is shooting at us in battle is evil. Wars are fought over land and territory, political gain, material wealth, and ideological differences; and they're usually instigated by leaders of governments. We have to realize that before a particular skirmish began, the individuals firing at us were not our enemies, nor will they be afterward. Just like us, these people were suddenly thrown into a conflict not of their making and told to destroy the enemy. These folks have families like we have; they eat, sleep, love, laugh, cry, and try to survive like we do; and most important, they are generally good like we are.

I think you get the point here . . . that war is one of humanity's most devastating follies. I can just see a soldier on the front lines having a buddy shot dead beside him and then yelling, "I love you!" as he empties his gun into the enemy. It's all so hypocritical and pointless. . . . I really don't consider war to be a good example of what "enemy" means, yet it is the most devastating to many innocent human beings.

Let's look at the word *enemy* as it should be defined. A true enemy is someone who knows you and, with malice aforethought, intends to hurt or destroy you. I'm not talking about a terrorist who's been brainwashed to annihilate any and all in the Western world—that's just some poor zealot being used by dark entities who, in their lunacy, want to wreak devastation and chaos. No, I'm talking about the individual who's part of your life and is perhaps a rival in some way, be it on or off the job. It's this type of person who is your real enemy . . . and yes, he or she will creep into your life like a thief in the night.

Now let's get back to the original premise of "Love your enemy." We all have our likes and dislikes, so co-workers and acquaintances will naturally fall into both of these categories. Since we're human, we're going to clash with those personalities we don't care for. However, the interesting thing is that we can love people's souls because they were created by Mother and Father God, but we don't have to like them or like their actions. Think about this for a moment: We love our Creators; correspondingly, we should try to love Their creations just as They do. They love all of us unconditionally, despite our shortcomings, because They created us. While we may not be able to attain this type of love, we can certainly give it the old college try.

What this means is that even though we're not fond of particular individuals, we can still love the soul within. The part of us that dislikes them is balanced by our ability to rise above our human emotions and love those people, regardless of their personalities or actions. (We do this very thing when we're on the Other Side, except we really don't have any negative emotions about anybody over there.)

The problem with taking "Love your enemy" literally is that in doing so, you're not loving *yourself*—you end up flying in the face of danger and then possibly becoming a doormat, which just about anyone who loves has been guilty of. You also leave yourself wide open to hypocrisy; after all, if you claim that you love Osama bin Laden but know in your heart that you could take a gun and shoot him for what he's done, then you're not being honest with yourself. But if you say, "I love the soul of Osama, but I intensely dislike him and his actions," you're being truthful, as well as allowing yourself to be human. If you don't allow yourself to be human, you'll find that it leads to hypocrisy and guilt . . . and you don't want or need that.

As for mystical travelers, they can carry a lot on their backs, but they seem to have an internal siren that warns them when enough is enough. They're "life's innkeepers" and want to feed and care for everyone, but they can't tend to those who are bent on destruction—they have to allow such individuals to go through their charts. Advanced entities realize that unlike them, many people haven't given up their will to God, so they still have a lot of learning to go through. They also realize that some learn quickly, while others do so at a slower pace.

There are so many souls waiting to be led out of the darkness—not necessarily to become mission-life entities or mystical travelers—but rather to find their own spiritual path. Most of all, they need to know that it's hell down here and that we all try the best we can to help each other through it.

Although unconditional love isn't always returned by the ones we give it to, it surely comes back from others if we're astute enough to see it. Love never dissipates; instead, it grows and comes back to us from everywhere.

✝ ✝ ✝

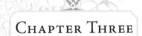

# CHAPTER THREE

# A COVENANT WITH GOD

Mystical travelers can be members of any faith—while the mantle takes precedence over any particular denomination, it won't keep them from belonging to it. All religious writings, and even the Ark of the Covenant, are forms of a sacred commitment to God. Thus, the oath of mystical travelers is their "ark," so to speak, or what the Bible refers to as a "covenant" with God. The oath is the highest form of commitment between human beings and the Divine.

Someone once asked Francine when we might see or feel any changes after accepting the mantle of the mystical traveler. She replied, "Almost immediately, a sense of peace and completion descends. Because you've given your life to the Higher Power, it begins to pull you, and so many things are revealed. Each day you feel that more and more is infused into you—it's like searching in the darkness, and then all of a sudden, the lights come on.

"Don't worry about your sincerity," she continued. "Just the fact that you have the courage to say the words of commitment is enough. You never have to second-guess God, even if you're afraid that you can't live up to your oath. The courage and satisfaction in doing God's work will be given to you. And please remember this, which I cannot stress too strongly: Once the mantle is dropped, it will never be removed."

My spirit guide states that as far back as records go, there has never been a mystical traveler who resented or didn't want his or her mantle. There have been many advanced souls who didn't use the term *mystical traveler,* but they didn't need to know the title to be included.

How many times have you met people, and you can't explain it, but they shine with such a brilliance that you feel you're part of them, and they you? Or what about those who, no matter what happens, know that God will take care of them and that they will prevail over all adversity? Well, they're all advanced entities, whether they realize it or not. Such individuals have a spiritual beeper that goes off so that everyone can hear it, as well as a need to serve others that simply becomes second nature.

For example, my church has started a school sanctioned by the government to teach people to become hypnotherapists, and we'd like to create one for children, as well as a place for the elderly. Yes, all this takes time and money, but I feel that it gives more honor to God than a large ornate cathedral would, especially if we only used it to worship on Sundays. We give to charities such as the Montel Williams MS Foundation and the Make-a-Wish Foundation, and we donate hundreds of toys and lots of food—all of which also honors God.

I'm not trying to say, "Look at us, aren't we holy and good!" I only mention these works because they're just a few examples of what some committed souls can do, and it's small compared to the efforts of others. But as Francine and I have always said, it's what you can do within your own resources and framework that matters.

Mystical travelers don't have to start churches or foundations, although some do. They also open schools, hospices, and medical clinics; and they give away resources, including their time and energy, wherever they're needed. What's most important is that they're consistent in the way they live good lives and love God.

We can find mystical travelers in politics, science, ecology, and even the celebrity world. They can be anywhere and in any occupation, as long as they're living out their lives in service to God and making a difference in the world, be it in a big or small way. Even those who are toiling in hospices, taking care of disabled children, tending the elderly, or simply living a life of sacrifice for others are lighting candles of spirituality for all they can . . . which is the mark of the mystical traveler.

### God's Powerful Programmers

Advanced souls can feel righteous anger when gross injustices are committed, but they never act out of violence. While they're the "spiritual SWAT team," or the "Green Berets of the universe," they don't carry weaponry or do harm to anyone—quite the contrary. Mystical travelers hate useless bloodshed, and work more on the soul level of helping others find peace and comfort in truth. However, they're not ethereal or mystical—they talk with candor and are grounded in reality. You'll never see them sitting and just contemplating the universe, for they're activators, teachers, writers, caretakers, and doers. They lead exemplary lives, having pledged to bring other people to light and love and to think for themselves.

Some of life's roads are extremely bumpy, so in certain situations, mystical travelers can say, "God, handle this." That is, sometimes they have to let go and let God take it or make it right . . . but not until they've tried everything else. Otherwise, they would never learn, and would instead just lie around and expect God to do everything for them.

Advanced entities do find that a great deal of any chronic illnesses they may have begins to diminish. This is not a cure-all because they did pick their charts and can't totally disturb them; rather, they just "rise above" the human body. They're powerful programmers because they have access to premonition, healing, and the ability to call on all the angels and the Mother God. Of course, everyone has these powers, but since mystical travelers have given up so much of life, they seem to come to the head of the line. Don't let this upset you, though: No matter who you are, you're still in line, and our Parents listen to everyone. In no way do I want you to feel that They play favorites.

## Using Magic

Speaking of programming, let's now discuss what might seem to be a very esoteric subject at first. It seems that mystical travelers become the masters of what's been called "imitative magic." This is a form of programming that ancient people were particularly fond of. They'd imitate what they wanted or needed from the gods by pouring pitchers of water on the ground and hoping for rain, and so forth.

Although mystical travelers are wonderful programmers, you can do the very same thing. In his book *The Power of Intention,* Dr. Wayne Dyer expertly writes that what you think and how you act will come to pass . . . it's truly the law of attraction. Try it yourself: Act as if you're happy, and happiness will come. Act as if you're well, and your body will follow suit. Act as if you have enough money (without going in debt), and you'll enjoy prosperity. On the other hand, if you act sick, depressed, run-down, or poor, you will have dug a hole where no light can come through.

You may ask, "But if you've written suffering into your chart, how do you change that?" You don't, but you can modify or shorten what's been written. Let's take the 24-hour flu as an example. I've been just as guilty of this, but did you ever notice that, as sure as the sun will rise, when you count off the time and reach the 24th hour, you feel fine? So why can't we have a 15-minute flu or just one week of cancer?

God love doctors, but they program us, too. For instance, I saw a woman on TV this morning who had brain cancer. The medical world had given her three months to live, yet she's now in her ninth year of being cancer free. She wouldn't listen to the statistics she'd been given and started to *live,* instead of merely waiting around for death. She wasn't necessarily a mystical traveler, as each and every one of us can heal and program ourselves.

It's very important to write down what you're programming for—whether it's health, well-being, love, wealth, or whatever you like—because the pen is mightier than the sword. The practice of writing also helps to implant what you want more strongly in your mind. The entire act uses your senses of touch and sight, and the more senses and faculties that you bring into play, the greater the impact the programming will have. Advertisers and masters of propaganda know that these are the techniques that make a greater impact on the human mind. So to have the greatest impact on your *own* mind, try to read your programming out loud every day, and it will sink into your very being.

### Soldiers for Azna

Francine says that mystical travelers dedicate their lives to Mother and Father God, but they also do it for their own advancement of soul. In other words, They never demanded it from these individuals. As They are just pure love and forgiveness, They don't demand *anything* from us—it's more the part of Them within us wanting to show our love by living our lives for Them.

If anything, mystical travelers are more like knights or soldiers for Azna (Mother God), because she takes more of a "hands on" approach to creation. Does that mean you're less in Her eyes (or, for that matter, our Father's eyes) if you're not a mystical traveler? Of course not! Advanced entities have decided to be the generals of the army of light down here, but they don't expect any medals. Again, what they do is for the advancement of their souls and because they love our Parents.

Father God is more static in nature, and it is His energy that holds all of creation together. He is the "unmoved mover," the Prima Mobile. Mother God, on the other hand, moves freely and gets involved with Their creations more. As She can intervene in our charts, She is the miracle worker. Before we come into life, She will even discuss with us the possibility of our becoming mystical travelers. We can argue with Her because we have freewill choice, but She usually prevails—Her loving persuasion makes us want to advance for Her. Then, with the help of the Council, we map out what roads we're going to take to fulfill our personal levels of perfection.

Right now I'd like you to take a moment to put yourself in front of your co-Creator, the all-loving and wonderful Mother God, and feel Her fantastic loving energy and power. Admit that you could never say no to Her, no matter what She asked of you. No one who is in their right mind could ever refuse Her anything . . . so you can now stop wondering how I became a mystical traveler.

### My Own Journey

I think what finally made taking the oath an easy decision for me (although I still had some trepidation) is the fact that my second husband had been conned into investing in a crooked gold-mining deal. I was so busy with my foundation that I really didn't have my mind on anything else but taking care of other people.

I was forced into bankruptcy, instructed to make restitution to the other investors, and had to pay off a huge IRS bill. I'll never forget the judge telling me, "I'm sorry, Mrs. Browne, but you're the only one making the money."

That night, I went into my bedroom and said, "God, You can take it all. It's Your will . . . but please just let me keep my foundation intact."

I lost my house and almost everything I owned. I was also taking care of my parents, so it was vital that I settle the whole matter. I needed $2,200 for housing, so I had a huge garage sale. I made $2,300 and put us all in the same modest apartment complex. My husband and I separated, and I eventually filed for divorce. Even though it was amicable, it was somewhat tragic in that we'd been together for almost 20 years. But, as he admitted, it was his fault;

in addition, he knew that I was devastated over the bankruptcy and only wanted me to be happy.

Although my second husband was not like my first (a terribly abusive man who beat me, mistreated our two boys, and even threatened my life), a divorce is a divorce and hard to go through. Happily, we've remained friends, and I have forgiven him . . . but I'm not sure that he'll ever forgive himself.

Anyway, after telling Mother and Father God They could have it all, I began to wonder what the difference was between that and becoming a mystical traveler. I reasoned that becoming such an advanced soul could even help make my life better, and I was right. It seemed insurmountable, but day after day and month after month, I built my life back by doing 25 to 30 readings a day. It wasn't the readings that wore me out, it was the worry that I wouldn't make it—but I did.

People have asked me, "If you're so psychic, why didn't you know all this was going to happen?" or "Why didn't Francine warn you?" The answer is simple: My gift has never been for *me*. And who's to say that without hitting bottom, it wouldn't have been harder to make my sacred commitment? After all, that's when I realized, down to the very depths of my soul, that God's will and mine are the same.

☩

A little while after I reestablished my work and finances, my church was in full swing, and Francine disseminated information on becoming a mystical traveler. She shared it with any members of the congregation who were interested over many weeks at my home base in Campbell, California, as well as in Seattle. It was during this period that several ministers and I took our oaths.

Not long after this, I lost nine people in about three months. My father; my mother; and several friends, including a doctor who'd been with me for years, just passed away one after the other. I know in my soul that I couldn't have gotten through that horrendous time of grief without the extra grace the mantle afforded me.

I'd also gotten married to my third husband, a man I'd known for 33 years and trusted for more than 20 in my organizations. A few years into our marriage, he took off with another woman when they were both with me on a "spiritual trip" to Egypt. Abass, a loving friend and tour operator who had taken us on many journeys to that beautiful country, called me every day to see if I was all right.

During one of our talks, I warned him not to go to Peru, but he was determined because he needed the money. I said, "Well, if you must go, don't climb," because I was worried about his heart. You guessed it: He climbed, came back to his hotel room, and dropped dead of a heart attack. So again, I found myself alone and feeling rejected.

I filed for divorce from my third husband; in the process, I discovered that he couldn't stand that I was more dedicated to my family and other people than I was to him, even though he'd known what my life was about before he married me. He also took money from me, but the adultery and deceit were the hardest to bear. Then, right in the middle of this debacle, both of my sons got divorced, too. It was almost like a giant psychic attack, and at times I felt that I couldn't breathe. I was numb with the betrayal and pain that surrounded me, but I held the mantle tightly around me.

I won't tell you it was instantaneous, but I did come out of this atrocious time so much stronger, especially with Montel Williams's support. We always know when the other is in trouble. Yet he was having his own pain during this time (the press is cruel and makes things up or twists them around, and all of us have to live with that). What I'm trying to drive home here is that no matter what crucifixion you go through—and it truly is like your soul being ripped apart—your knowledge and faith will strengthen you physically, mentally, and especially spiritually.

Tragically, my last husband ended up getting throat cancer. I'm not presumptuous enough to think that it was karma, nor would I truly wish anyone any harm, but it's so clear that what goes around comes around. Yet I had deep sorrow and even prayed that he'd make it. Although I kid and make jokes about some of the tragedies in my life, such as saying after he left me that I wanted to run over him and that woman with a Mack truck, that was just me trying to ease my very human pain by making light of things.

All of these incidents circled around to make me stronger and show me that I have to be the captain of my own ship. I realized that my love affair is with all of you and the world, through my writing, teaching, and lecturing. My family, my friends, my pets, and my travels are the loves of my all-encompassing and fulfilling life.

So even though I had some hesitation, I'd never, ever think of giving up my mantle. Even as hard as life has been, the spiritual gains have far outweighed everything else. If you're suffering or in a desert period right now, know that becoming a mystical traveler is no quick or miraculous fix—but boy, you do get through it with so much more strength, knowledge, and fortitude. You'll find that all of the hardships you suffer only expand your soul; and joy blossoms like flowers blooming after a long, cold winter.

### Just Between You and God

I think a lot of the apprehension you might feel about becoming a mystical traveler stems from the same fear I had: that God's will is in opposition to yours. Well, take comfort in the fact that God's will does take precedence, but it won't interrupt your life or loves or even likes. You won't suddenly become someone else, and no one will know what's happened but you. However, others *will* note that there's something different about you . . . there's a light or a sort of sanctity that they can't put their finger on, but for lack of a better phrase, they'll see a better you!

When you take on the mantle, you can't drink, eat, take, or do anything in excess that will harm your body, including drugs. I don't mean prescriptions for illness, as long as these pills are not overused. Taking too much of any substance is a slow way of killing yourself, and the use of recreational drugs is madness and stupidity. Although, like in the case of Anna Nicole Smith, sometimes it's hard to know who's to blame: the person taking all the drugs, or the doctors who prescribed them. Either way, we can't judge what kind of life or weakness or pain such an individual is carrying, or know how he or she is going to react when thrust into the limelight.

As for Ms. Smith herself, she was probably warned by the Council when she wrote her chart that she may be going in too soon or that her soul was too fragile for the life she'd laid out for herself. The Anna Nicole Smiths, Marilyn Monroes, and Elvis Presleys of this world of course make it to the Other Side, but they seem to allow themselves to be put into the hands of shady puppet masters before they get there. They then turn inward and become so full of fear and rejection that they simply can't handle it. We can only feel tremendous sorrow for these poor souls—especially since it's likely that in some life, we all jumped in too fast or picked too hastily.

The good news is that all of your bad or unhealthy habits seem to disappear or can be broken almost immediately when you become a mystical traveler. But that doesn't mean that you must become overly scrupulous: You don't have to stop everything or suddenly become a vegan, unless you want to. You don't need to dress differently, change your hairstyle, or become plain and nondescript.

I drink coffee, get my hair and nails done (yes, they're mine), and I do wear some makeup. However, I only tend to do so when I'm onstage, on TV, or going to some social function, because it makes me feel like I'm wearing a mask otherwise. Yet even when I'm at home doing readings or writing, I don't walk around without any pride about how I look.

I think the old adage of "moderation in all things" is right, and it doesn't just point to what we ingest—it also cautions us against being frivolous with money, speech, or actions. I do like to gamble a little and I love to shop, but I don't spend too much or go on binges. If you do anything to excess, it can be so nerve-wracking that it greatly impacts your pocketbook *and* your health.

⚜

You should never be running around telling people that you're a mystical traveler, for it's a quiet oath between you and God, and no one keeps track of you except *you*.

I'd like to change the subject for a minute here to warn you about any organization, society, or church that is controlling. Once you get into such a group, it becomes occult. I just saw an association on TV that watches what its members weigh, what they eat, what medicines they take, where they go, and what they say. Please don't walk away from something like this—run! We're going to see these types of groups cropping up everywhere, and if there's anything close to an antispiritual movement, it's this. Be discerning and cautious of anyone taking over your life; your soul is only between you and God, and no one else.

That's why I'm so paranoid and repeatedly say, "Take with you what you want and leave the rest behind." I simply put forth truthful information as I know it to be, and you can either reject or accept it. I know that all of the teachings and philosophies I share are infused by God. I also know that the soul recognizes the truth . . . but it may not be ready for it.

Finally, I ask that you keep in mind these words from Francine: "God is in service to us. We are in service to God. Each of us is in service to each other . . . that makes us whole." You may have a hard time with the first part of the sentence, but it's true. Our Parents give us the option of paying homage to Them through our actions; in doing so, we get service and help from Them. Simply put—we're never left alone by our all-loving and forgiving Creators.

I know that it can be hard to go against thousands of years of tradition and programming to get at what's real, but once you do, you'll discover so much. You'll realize that these long-hidden truths help your soul become so much more peaceful, yet invigo-rated, because you're finally getting logical and honest answers to your questions.

✝ ✝ ✝

# CHAPTER FOUR

# DOGMA, DHARMA, AND KARMA

Propaganda can be a very powerful tool. Entire governments in Russia and Nazi Germany once used it very effectively, and it's still being utilized in China and North Korea. In the United States, we see how advertising agencies and the media employ it every day. As for so-called journalists, they seem to always follow the old axiom of "bad news makes headlines," so a tragic story is like money in the bank.

Propaganda works so well because it basically programs the human mind, so you always need to be aware of what types of messages you're receiving—especially when it comes to religion and society. When you're subjected to continual negative programming, it has such an effect on your soul that it can hamper its spiritual growth.

If you go to a church, synagogue, temple, or mosque, really listen and find out whether your religious leader tends to stress the negative or the positive. If it's the latter, you can take joy in your faith and truly worship God in the way you want. But if it's the former, watch out. Be aware that you're being programmed with negativity such as bigotry (sermons should never put down other beliefs or certain practices); the fear of God (remember that our Creators are only loving and merciful); guilt (be wary if everyone is called a "sinner" or "unworthy," if you're told that your soul will not be saved unless you do such and such, or if you're asked for money over and over again); and hypocrisy (no one dogma or creed is the only way to salvation).

Any religion that isn't magnanimous or tolerant of other belief systems, or even other sects of the same faith, can be very negative and certainly give you a false sense of what spirituality really is. Protect yourself by paying attention to anything that seems like propaganda trying to brainwash you. Above all, try to keep it simple by just loving God with all your heart and soul and following the Golden Rule of doing to others as you would have them do to you. True spirituality is basic and complete, and anyone can attain it, despite religious traditions and society's tainted preponderance for wealth and power.

Unfortunately, too many people equate spirituality with religion. Many go to church and think that they're spiritual for doing so; and indeed, some are. To practice your faith is fine and good, but you must do so with pure motive and intent. Whenever it becomes an obligation rather than a joy, spirituality goes out the window. Being devout is not just about going to Mass every Sunday or facing east to do prayers five times a day—it's really about being as much like God as you can be . . . and you don't have to follow any religion to do that.

The real key to being a spiritual person is trying to live *every day* in a spiritual manner. Going to church will not accomplish this, for it must come from within. In fact, Francine says that your church is inside your own body, soul, and mind because God is everywhere. A lot of people claim to accept spirituality, but they don't live by it. Of course we all make mistakes, but we readjust and walk the walk. If we don't—or if we fail to follow the two basic commandments of "Do unto others" and "Love God with all your heart and soul"—then we're not living the way every human being should.

Attaining spirituality is what's really meant by "Christ consciousness." "The Word made flesh" is nothing more than our Parents creating us, Their children, as part of Themselves and in Their image. All of us are "the Word of God," so to speak, which brought us into life so that we could glorify and learn. We can be messengers to neutralize the energy on this negative and temporary plane of existence; that is, we can be pillars of light to shine in the darkness. If we're sent to places and we don't understand why, we'll soon figure out that it's to plant light columns of spiritual knowledge . . . ultimately, we'll realize that we *are* the light columns.

### Fear and Misconceptions

The whole concept of seeking spirituality is a calling, in a sense. We see so many people who have answered that calling by becoming priests, preachers, monks, or nuns; while others do volunteer work, protest against injustice, or contribute to various charities. Most are successful and are to be commended, but for some others, their activities are just covering up hypocrisy.

Hypocrisy is a subject that Jesus talked about at length, and it's one of the greatest traps we'll encounter in life. If we think about it, we'll see that our whole society is saddled with it in many ways. Religion is particularly full of hypocrisy, especially when it's taken to its extremes; for example, it preaches "Love thy neighbor" and then instigates wars and terrorism. The Catholic Church admits its many atrocities (yet apologizes with little fanfare), but then it turns around and says that the Pope is infallible. The Catholic and Protestant faiths preach against homosexuality and "sinful" sexual practices—spouting bigotry and instigating hate crimes—only to be party to all sorts of scandals involving pastors, preachers, and priests that are sexual in nature. As Rodney King so famously asked, "Can we all get along?"

Organized religion has one basic and big problem: It has gathered so much human-made dogma that it's trapped itself within its own rules and regulations. Instead of putting out God's word in a simple manner, the leaders complicate it with what *they* feel is decent human behavior, and the pieces often don't fit or end up causing more problems than they solve.

I'm constantly amazed by how many people listen to, and even blindly follow, those who are supposedly in service to God yet only sermonize about hellfire and brimstone. You know the type—the evangelistic and ultraconservative preachers who are always hammering away about a wrathful, vengeful, and punishing God Who is going to send you to everlasting damnation unless you follow what *they* say. These tend to be men (although there are some women, too) who regularly stress fear in order to keep their flocks under their control and contributing to their coffers. "Satan" or "the devil" is seemingly in every other sentence, and demons that possess or cause us to go astray are continually being brought up. Doesn't anyone think logically or clearly when they're part of these congregations?

Educated people usually know when psychological tools are being used to try to control them, but I've known *highly* educated individuals who seemed to toss their brains away as soon as they got to these types of churches or evangelical tent shows. I know I'm on a soapbox here, but I get so angry when I see how these supposed men of God perpetuate negativity all the time. All they're doing is taking humankind's innate fear of the unknown and utilizing it to their advantage. It's sad and wrong . . . and takes us back to the Dark Ages, when people were burned at the stake.

For some awful reason, religion has generally concentrated its efforts on emphasizing negativity and punishment instead of trying to soothe people with positive thoughts and by affirming God's goodness and love. I suppose it's because those in charge think that everyone is prone to "temptation" and "sinful ways," and that human nature, being what it is, will gravitate toward negative behavior. The plain and simple truth is that this planet *is* negative in nature, and we all face darkness every day of our lives. But instead of trying to alleviate that darkness through love and positive messages, religion just adds to the negativity. And in all of this, to misrepresent God and Jesus Christ is the greatest tragedy of all.

So many times I've heard preachers and other religious experts claim: "Jesus said this, but what he really meant was that." No, he didn't. Francine insists that Jesus said what he meant and did what he was supposed to do, without any hidden or double meanings. And he never claimed that he came to die for our sins—Paul inserted that many years after the Crucifixion when he wrote his Epistles. (As an aside, I just hate it when overly zealous followers put words in the mouth of the one they've been following after he or she dies and then pronounce it as fact.)

Paul, a zealot if there ever was one, never met Christ . . . and neither did the writers of the four canonical Gospels that are attributed to Matthew, Mark, Luke, and John. Biblical scholars know that these Gospels were authored many years after the Crucifixion, but that fact is not highly publicized. As a result, a lot of people believe that they were actually written by the apostles (which they weren't) and that Paul was himself an apostle (which he never was).

Why does the Christian faith perpetuate such falsehoods to this day? Because the early church leaders chose to be *apostolic,* meaning that they follow the teachings of the apostles. For all intents and purposes, they even chose to make Paul an apostle— after all, Christianity definitely follows his instructions more than any other, including those of Jesus himself.

When the battle between early Christian factions was finally over, Pauline (related to Paul) Christianity won out, making it the most widely practiced form of Christianity today. So when you get right down to it, Christian teachings are the result of writings by Paul and some obscure monks who penned the four Gospels. Throw in the essay on the political machinations of Roman rule that's now known as "the Book of Revelation," and presto! You have what we call the New Testament . . . sad, but true.

I certainly don't mean to be glib about this, but I've always maintained that the Bible can be both inspirational and very dangerous. So much of it is allegorical in nature, yet it is interpreted literally. It is oftentimes called "the Word of God," but biblical scholars know full well that it was written by human beings.

I also find it funny that many Christians incorporate the Old Testament in their teachings, but then they turn around and condemn the Judaic faith. Christ was a Jew; but he came to change many of the Jewish outlooks, traditions, and laws by preaching about an all-loving, all-merciful, and all-forgiving God. These teachings more or less evolved into the Christian faith, despite all the alterations and misinterpretations that those who followed him perpetuated.

### Keeping Our Faith

I know it must seem that I'm being repetitious at times when I discuss a few of these topics, but it's because I have such an aversion to the tactics of those who try to convert or control other people. I get so tired of evangelists and conservative churches using God as a weapon of intimidation and fear. To them, all people are sinners and are prevented from getting into heaven unless they follow certain teachings—and, above all, support a certain ministry by donating money. Their fund-raising and tithing methods can be reprehensible and remind me of the old indulgence practices of the Catholic Church. There's nothing wrong with receiving compensation for work done, but expecting people to part with cash they don't have in the name of "salvation" or to secure their place in heaven is depraved and greedy.

You hear such individuals say, "You won't be saved [or enter the kingdom of heaven] unless you give," or "Support our ministry and we'll pray for you to be forgiven of your sins." They also use other methods of fear: They might tell you that you have a demon in you, for instance, and the only way to be saved is to donate money or follow their teachings. It seems that everything is based on sin, hell, the devil, and a wrathful God. I've seen so much of this, and I've had enough. I believe to the core of my soul that you can give people tools and guidance, but you should *never* tell them that your way is the only way.

Sure, I'd love for all of you to become members of my church and believe 100 percent in what I say, but that's not very realistic. I put forth what I know to be true, but my truth may not be yours, or you might not choose to buy into everything I do. I just try to help whomever I can, but it's certainly not mandatory that you subscribe to all of my beliefs. I'd never tell those who disagreed with me that they're damned or will be "left behind." No one could ever be left behind because they didn't believe in Jesus, let's say. After all, Mohammed and Buddha were also true messengers of God.

I think that through simply being spiritual, no matter what group or creed you align with, you're truthfully taking a shortcut to your goal of spiritual evolvement. Yes, I am a Christian because that's my preference, but Christianity is not the only belief system that adores, loves, and gives honor to God; and if I were a Buddhist, Muslim, Jew, or Hindu, I'd never feel that our all-loving Creators would be so capricious and humanized as to play favorites. If They made *everyone,* how could They?

Logic alone tells us that most religions are misinformed or incorrect if their dogmas insist that we'll be damned to some hell if we don't believe the way they do, and the use of fear has no place in true spirituality. No one, *absolutely no one,* will be left behind— it's cruel and elitist to think that only a select group will be saved, while the rest of the millions of souls (whom God also made) will be relegated to some form of hell and everlasting punishment.

Many fundamentalists won't even let their followers read other religious works. With fundamentalist Christians, only the Bible is allowed; with fundamentalist Muslims, it's the Koran. Those in charge like to say that reading other spiritual books will spread corruption because these works are evil and untrue—but if they're so sure that they're right, these people should let their flocks read *everything.* I mean, you'd think that if they were secure in their beliefs, they'd allow their members to read whatever they want . . . but perhaps the reason why they don't allow it is because they're actually very insecure. I guess the best defense for their beliefs is a potent offense of fear and damnation for those who don't follow their teachings.

In addition, within the framework of religions such as Christianity and Islam are very conservative sects, which state that those who don't follow their precepts will not be saved or have any chance to go to the Other Side. Think about it . . . this means that Moses and everyone in the Old Testament didn't get to go Home because they weren't Christian or Muslim. Now, granted, I'm being a little bit extreme here; and both Christianity and Islam do give homage to their Jewish predecessors, but what about all the thousands of people who have never heard of Christ or Mohammed? What about the good and holy folks who follow a different faith? Many of these individuals are doing more good works and helping more people than the rest of us on Earth are.

None of this makes any sense unless you realize that both Christianity and Islam are battling for converts, and the demands on their followers will only get worse as the fear of losing them increases. Islam is the fastest growing religion in the world today; while Christianity may be losing members, it's fighting back hard. Mark my words, this "war" between the two biggest faiths in the world is going to heat up, and both are going to become more intolerant—especially of each other. It is so tragic.

✟

I know I'm back on my soapbox and getting a bit preachy, but it's only to get you to think logically as well as spiritually. Anyone who insists, "I'm the best!" is into prejudging others and its inevitable by-product: bigotry.

Just today I spoke to a woman on the phone who was in hysterics because her four children had decided to become Buddhists. She was so concerned that they either wouldn't be saved or were irretrievably lost. I asked her where she ever got the idea that God didn't make Buddha, too—what made her think that he wasn't a mystical traveler as well? After all, such advanced souls are found in every walk of life and in every religion.

Please take a moment to read the Beatitudes, which Jesus gave in his Sermon on the Mount:

*Blessed are the poor in spirit: for theirs is the kingdom of heaven.*

*Blessed are they that mourn: for they shall be comforted.*

*Blessed are the meek: for they shall inherit the earth.*

*Blessed are they which do hunger and thirst after righteousness: for they shall be filled.*

*Blessed are the merciful: for they shall obtain mercy.*

*Blessed are the pure in heart: for they shall see God.*

*Blessed are the peacemakers: for they shall be called the children of God.*

*Blessed are they which are persecuted for righteousness' sake: for theirs is the kingdom of heaven.*

*Blessed are ye, when men shall revile you, and persecute you, and shall say all manner of evil against you falsely, for my sake.*

*Rejoice, and be exceeding glad: for great is your reward in heaven: for so persecuted they the prophets which were before you* (Matthew 5:3–12).

Now compare that to Buddha's Noble Eightfold Path, which is divided into three basic categories: wisdom (right view and right intention); ethical conduct (right speech, right action, and right livelihood); and mental discipline (right effort, right mindfulness, and right concentration). Do you see how similar in spirit they are?

When they started, most religions weren't religions at all; rather, they were spiritual messages that mystical travelers such as

Jesus and Buddha put out and hoped that people would embrace. As I've asked many people over the years, how could Christ be Christian? What did he do . . . follow himself?

As you can see, those who only adhere to one creed or read one religious book become very narrow-minded; they then find themselves in a position of not being able to question what they're told. As mystical travelers, we can never damn or judge such individuals, but we can feel sorry that they're unable to experience many different types of thought, ideas, and philosophies. I've always said that I *judge the action of judging.* Francine has told me that she really likes this phrase, and many of those on the Other Side are using it now.

A research group once asked my other guide, Raheim, "How can we cleanse human-made dogma?"

He answered, "You, as spiritual entities, must always profess against it. You will never eliminate it, for it is part of the negativity of this planet; as such, it is a learning experience from which people can either break away from or be sucked into. Spiritual entities always break away from such constricting and illogical dogma— but as with most of life, it is a test. Those who are sucked into these dogmas will find it very hard to advance the spirituality of their souls."

### Returning to Gnosis

I don't care if you live to be 200 (who would want to?), this planet isn't your eternal home. It's only a transitory place to learn and, as I've said many times, a bad camping trip at best. But those of us who have incarnated can live with joy and take a great amount of comfort in the truth of why we're here and where we're going, thus leaving all the human moneymaking dogma behind. Life is not easy because it does give us a sense of aloneness, futility, and absence from God, but knowing the truth makes it a lot easier.

And once we adopt a Gnostic viewpoint, we become free of guilt, a hateful and condemning God, and so forth. *Gnosticism* is just a word that means that a soul's journey includes seeking a loving Father *and* Mother, as well as knowing that our time here on Earth is short and is to be spent learning for Them. We believe, as Christ did, that "my kingdom is not of this world."

By living so many lives, you're able to have all types of experiences for God. All the human joys and heartaches within those existences make up the manner in which you bring yourself to gnosis. *Gnosis* means that you learn for yourself to advance yourself—it's the search for your own truth. Gnosis is so broad and universal that people on their last lives come to thoroughly understand the simple message that Jesus and other messengers taught: *Love God, do good, and then you go Home to the Other Side.*

What's remarkable is that when you look back to the time before formal religion took hold, all entities in life got this gnosis. Sure, they might have prayed to the Sun God or tried to appease the God of Rain or the God of the Volcano with sacrifices, but they were simplistic in their everyday dealings. Ancient Greek philosophers had this simplicity; children still have it innately today, at least until someone comes along to screw them up. (By the same token, kids often remember their past lives and see their guides and passed-over loved ones, but as they grow older, they lose the ability because other people tell them it's not real.)

Then a ripple happened in which the paternal leaders took hold and began to talk for God or Jesus or whoever the messenger was. Thus, if anyone tried to put forth the Gnostics' philosophy, they were often deemed to be heretics and killed. Look at the thousands of women murdered for being "witches," even when they were actually healers; the scientists who were put to death for saying that the world was not flat or the earth rotated around the sun; and the like.

At that time, the powers that be wanted to suppress all new thinking, and their fervor led to actions such as the burning of the Library of Alexandria. I happen to feel that this was one of the most horrible atrocities in human history because we lost so much knowledge in that one single act. Francine says the library contained books that carried information about UFOs and the alien influence on Earth's early cultures; as well as great philosophical, spiritual, and historical works that are now lost forever. (Thankfully, copies of them exist on the Other Side.)

In times long past, average men and women only had oral traditions, which is why we don't have much that remains in the way of written works from ancient cultures. People were not encouraged to read and write because rulers and religious leaders wanted power over their subjects. The more you research for yourself, the more you can make your own Gnostic reasoning. And that's what the mystical travelers are here for: to spread light *and* enlightenment.

☩

Mystical travelers can get married, have children, run businesses, and live lives outside the confines of an abbey, a monastery, or a convent. The reason why the Catholic Church ruled out marriage for priests and nuns was purely financial—that is, they didn't want to support any families. In the early days of the faith, women were like priests, doling out spiritual advice, and the priests themselves could marry and have families. History bears out that some Popes were married and had children: Even Pope Pius XII had a nun he lived with, whom many insiders called "the Popessa." Why would God care if we procreated? Isn't one of the reasons we decide to come down to learn is that we can create vehicles for others to come into?

The Church is also against birth control, which, of course, makes for more members. I used to wonder how it was that priests couldn't have children, yet they could make it dogma for everyone else to have as many as they could. There's also a rule that if a pregnant woman is in danger of dying, you save the baby first and let the mother die. I used to argue with priests and nuns about this until I was blue in the face, although many didn't want to get into it, just saying that it is what it is. I'd then come back with, "But Jesus never said—" At that point, I'd promptly be interrupted and told very firmly, "That's enough, Sylvia." I'm not just picking on Catholicism, though, because other religions have similar ridiculous human-made rules.

# Dogma, Dharma, and Karma

You have to have some uniformity, as we do in our Society of Novus Spiritus with our robes and colors, but that's only to let people know that we're Gnostics. Our services stay pure, and no one tells the congregation what to do or not to do . . . the spiritual information we give out is not dogmatic in any way, unlike many religions, which threaten you with hell or retribution if you break the rules.

As a mystical traveler, or even if you just want to elevate your knowledge and spirituality, you should read and research not only the Bible, but also the Talmud, the Koran, the Bhagavad Gita, the Egyptian Book of the Dead, Buddhist scriptures, and so forth. You'll find that many of these works can be beautiful in their simplicity. When you sift through them all, you'll discover that they lead to the same place: *Love God, don't hurt each other, and love your neighbor as yourself.*

Like the crusaders of old, mystical travelers come in and cut away the excess fat, as it were. As strange as it may seem, they're never in a state of faith, but rather one of knowing. All entities, especially spiritual ones, come in with a big label that reads: Do GOOD AND AVOID EVIL. Of course this doesn't work if you sit back and let everyone tell you what to do or that God won't forgive you for something you did or didn't do.

No one judges you but you, and if you're a true Bible-following person, then God bless you. But whatever you adhere to, feel comfortable with it and embrace it with your whole heart. If you're a mystical traveler, you'll find that you must embrace all the good from every religion as well. For example, I have a mezuzah on the door of my house, while inside I have a head of the Buddha and other Buddhist statues; a painting of Krishna; several statues of Hindu gods, Kuan-yin, and the Virgin Mary; many crosses; and dozens of icons and paintings of Jesus. It looks like the home of many religions, which I love.

I feel that if someone can keep you in a box, then they have control over you. As Francine says, "Do not live by any norms except your own God center." And my quote has always been: "You are your own temple. You are the living Christ consciousness, and the Holy Spirit moves through you in this chaotic world."

### Dharma vs. Karma

There is often a great deal of confusion over the difference between karma and dharma. *Karma* is experiencing for God; and a small part of it is the belief that what goes around, comes around. In other words, if you create havoc or pain in someone's life, with the real purpose or motive to do so, it will come back to you. However, if you *inadvertently* hurt another, there will be no retribution.

Unlike what some people think, karma ends with each life. While we can carry over the cell memory of hurts and phobias and traumas from one life to another, we don't bring along karmic retribution. Where many get confused is when a soul doesn't accomplish all that it wanted to in a life, so it chooses another existence that's similar in order to complete its education. This is not karmic in nature; it's just finishing up the experience or lesson that the soul wanted to learn in the first place.

*Dharma,* on the other hand, is more the taking on of responsibility for your life and chart, and doing so with good conduct and virtue. Mystical travelers have a lot of dharma, but their charts don't get negated. Instead, they become more accented—the highs are higher, and the lows are lower.

A few aspects of dharma that you might take on as a mystical traveler are:

- Being a great parent who helps other boys and girls and/or families

- Caring for the elderly or young people

- Becoming a mother or father to foster children

- Bringing harmony into your family (unless they're dark entities)

- Writing spiritual works

- Being a priest- or nunlike entity who gives blessings and prays for people

- Teaching, preaching, or being a confidant to another

- Providing comfort to all those who come to you (as well as to yourself)

- Servicing humankind in any way, be it on a large or small scale

- Being a Giver of Life—that is, one who brings others hope and help and truth

You may say, "Well, I've done this," and most people have, but it's not as simplistic as it sounds. You must go beyond parenting your own child to get out in the community and reach other souls. In this way, you'll bring them knowledge of the love of our wonderful Creators, just as Jesus did.

✢ ✢ ✢

# CHAPTER FIVE

# NAMES
# WRITTEN
# IN GOLD

Francine says that once you accept the mantle of the mystical traveler, you can have a wonderful spiritual life forever. No longer are you concerned with social standing, wealth, materialism, longevity, and the like—you know that the Other Side is your eternal home and that this place called "Earth" is so transitory in comparison.

Of course you can still live well or enjoy the fruits of your honest labor, but they'll always take their place behind God's will and what your Parents want you to do. As an advanced soul, you're a spiritual pilgrim or pioneer; as time goes on and your work for Them has its influence, you'll no longer feel as if you're the only one on a lonely road, for others will step in line behind you or even walk with you.

According to my spirit guide, the names of all mystical travelers are written in gold on the Other Side. It's similar to the awards and honors that are given to students, philanthropists, entertainers, humanitarians, scientists, and so many others in every field of endeavor on this planet. Everyone aspires to some type of acknowledgment, and that doesn't stop when we get Home. Francine also says that acknowledgment of such entities brings about the greatest respect, which makes sense to me: Anyone who has worked tirelessly to elevate him- or herself and advance spiritually certainly deserves more acclaim than those who fall into apathy or mediocrity.

Francine goes on to state that whatever road you choose as a mystical traveler, you'll end up administering to others. While some human beings may help others because they like their work or the money it brings, what drives advanced entities is their desire to learn, advance, and work for God.

My guide once told some of the ministers in my church that after her instruction on mystical travelers was over, they could walk out and never come back—but they'd invariably find their own niche in which they could help people understand our all-loving Creators and do as much good as they could, even if it was only in modest ways. She explained that by helping others and performing even small acts of kindness, the integral parts of the foundation for becoming a mystical traveler would be in place.

As you know, to have the calling to be a mystical traveler usually takes about 20 years, but that does take your "pondering" time into consideration. "In your world," Francine explains, "everything has a time, but this is not so on the Other Side. In becoming a mystical traveler, there is often a time period in which you will not commit to doing so for 5, 10, 20, or more years. Sylvia herself carried her thrust toward being a mystical traveler for 20 years in incubation.

"Some of you may protest, 'But I just started.' No, you did not. As you sit and contemplate, you may be surprised to find that you began to question many years ago, perhaps as early as childhood. That was the birth of the spiritual you, even if it was only in your superconscious. And really, what does it matter how long it takes you to become a mystical traveler? As long as you choose to give up your will, it can happen on your deathbed."

In fact, my spirit guide says that we should never quit questioning or seeking or researching, for everyone continues to do so on the Other Side, where it's all about joy and discovery for all. No one ever knows everything over there, and the beauty is that all entities are constantly learning.

### *Life on the Other Side*

Please keep in mind that eternity is a long time, so the chance that we're all acquainted with one another on the Other Side is basically 100 percent. You must remember that we all came from the Divine Sparkler (which, of course, is God), so we've all known each other everywhere. You might think this is too much to hold or remember, but that's because we humans are lucky if we use one-tenth of our brains. When we're Home, our minds are working at full capacity, so we're aware of and can recall everything. To be with millions of souls we've known and loved is a glorious thing . . . not to mention being with Jesus, our guides, the angels, and Mother and Father God.

Truly, there are some whom we're closer to, just like best friends here on Earth. But we don't dislike anyone else because that type of negative human emotion doesn't exist on the Other Side, which is free of pettiness, greed, jealousy, and the like. While we do love everyone over there, we stick close to many of those souls whom we've shared lives with, or whom we felt a kinship with from the very beginning. Yes, we're the best version of ourselves when we're Home, but we still keep our individual personalities. Otherwise, we'd all be the same loving robots, which would be incredibly boring.

Each life has shaped our soul in a different way, not only from being in human form, but also from gaining the knowledge and experience that has formed who and what we are. That's why we recognize each other in this life and on the Other Side. "Birds of a feather do flock together," but we love, honor, and respect all of God's creations.

Some may be very surprised when they find that they can now understand all things better on the Other Side, even those individuals they couldn't fathom while on Earth. So again, be very careful about whom you judge—in fact, you shouldn't judge at all because what you see through your limited earthly viewpoint may be entirely different when perceived with the expanded vision of the Other Side.

Mystical travelers meet with each other every so often for the purposes of discussing their next missions, sharing their experiences, or exploring how they can improve . . . the same as old friends who have gone through so much together. In addition, they're known as some of the greatest teachers on the Other Side. Francine says that there are long intervals in between assignments in which these advanced souls are instructing and, of course, still learning. They read and research, but they also play or listen to music and attend social events to share experiences and knowledge with others. Never get the idea that they're better or more elite than anyone else, for they mix with all entities.

Mystical travelers only tend to "flock together" when they're on a special mission—the rest of the time you wouldn't be able to discern them from the other entities on the Other Side. In other words, they don't lord their status over everyone, get special privileges, wear a different form of clothing, don a pin, or what have you.

Entities on the sixth level who work in orientation and help incoming and outgoing souls are appreciated because of what they do, and it's the same with mystical travelers. However, no one on the Other Side is considered to be better than anyone else. It would be similar to going to a party on this side where everyone was happy and congenial and having a great time—I don't think anybody would care who pumped gas or who was a CEO.

All individuals have worth and are equal, especially as far as our Parents are concerned. As a matter of fact, sometimes what we think of as a lowly job is being done by some incredibly advanced souls . . . this is yet another example of why we truly can't "judge a book by its cover," nor can we classify people based on their professions. Earthly society tends to label men and women according to their stature and wealth, but on the Other Side, there is no such judgment because we're all equal.

The other day I was asked if we will all ultimately reside on this planet's Other Side. I answered that most of us will; however, others will choose to go to that of another world. The irony is that at the end of this reincarnation schematic, all of the Other Sides in existence will come together and become one huge Home.

When mystical travelers die, they're often called on to become spirit guides. Many times they're even asked to incarnate on other planets to bring about betterment through teaching or leading—not so much for their souls' advancement, but to gather data. Now it's true that all entities can visit other worlds and even live on them, but they're not the data gatherers that mystical travelers are. These advanced souls bring Home all this knowledge to share with everyone, and they also infuse it into people who are still alive on Earth.

The mystical travelers who come back from other planets with this knowledge are not considered extraterrestrials. They're "ultra-terrestrials," which means that they stay in their own spiritual and eternal form, just as all those who reside on the Other Side do. The term *extraterrestrial* is reserved for those souls who colonized this planet millions of years ago and visit to see what we humans have done with it in the meantime.

I often think that they must be very disappointed with how we've destroyed the streams and oceans, had countless wars, and perpetrated unbelievable horrors on one another. Yet I'm sure they will make themselves more and more known in less than ten years because "the veil" between our two worlds is becoming thinner all the time. As it finally disappears altogether, we won't just see the few ghosts that haven't made it back Home yet, but we'll also be able to perceive our passed-over loved ones, angels, spirit guides, and other advanced spiritual beings . . . and even the Other Side itself.

### The Truth about Soul Mates

Mystical travelers can have soul mates if *they* are also mystical travelers. If not, they stick with the many kindred souls who really can take the place of a soul mate. In fact, this seems like a good place to thoroughly address the soul-mate concept.

If you look at life, almost everything is in duality, so why wouldn't it be true of human beings as well? Yes, of course there is another half of you. You were created in duality as male and female, almost like twin souls. Consequently, there is another half of yourself in existence that's identical in every way, except it's of the opposite gender. The problem is that you're most likely inclined to try to find the other side of yourself—that all-encompassing soul mate—but the chances of your finding him or her in life are about 0.5 percent.

Even after all my years of readings, I could count on one hand those I've met whose soul mates were alive at the same time, and still have fingers left over. The reason it's so rare is because your soul mate generally stays on the Other Side to help protect you. You see, life is just too haphazard at times, and even written charts can take detours or different roads to finally reach their destinations. So if two soul mates incarnated at the same time on Earth, with all of its chaos and unpredictability, chances are that they'd never even meet (unless they came into the same family, which hardly ever happens). Soul mates find it more expedient to let only one of them incarnate at a time, rather than brave the crapshoot of possibly never meeting in life.

While the probability that your soul mate is on the Other Side is 99.5 percent, don't forget about kindred souls, who are just as important. As Francine says, "You may leave your soul mates for a while, but you have a mission to accomplish on some planet for God. You are always in contact with them; they come along with you like your guide, angels, and loved ones from life, as well as the Other Side." Yet she states that even when we're Home, we don't always stay with our soul mates all the time. While we were made as twins, kindred souls are as important to us as soul mates are. Mystical travelers, especially, find that they don't only stay with their twin souls, even if they're also mystical travelers—this is because they go on so many singular journeys for God that it takes them away quite a lot.

Mystical travelers usually don't work together that often unless there needs to be an earthshaking spiritual campaign started for God. In those instances you might see a number of advanced entities pulling together as one to establish a movement, cause, or belief that will have far-reaching effects on a planet. When this happens, you might see soul mates coming into life together, but this is extremely rare.

Even if our twin souls don't incarnate with us, we still have wonderful people with whom we can interact in life. We will all meet kindred souls on our eternal journey, and I'd personally find it very depressing to pine away for my soul mate and ignore all the loved ones I've met in this life, such as my ministers, children, friends, grandchildren, and even dearest animals.

You can form strong bonds between such individuals that rival those you form with your soul mate. Since your twin soul is probably not here with you in life, you'll realize that the love between kindred souls fills the void and greatly helps you to fulfill your goals of spirituality and evolvement.

✢ ✢ ✢

# CHAPTER SIX

# THE EIGHT GOLDEN KEYS OF KNOWLEDGE

Some of the most important tools we're given in life are called "the Eight Golden Keys of Knowledge," which point to the advancement of our souls. It may seem at times that to advance at all is impossible—but if you've at least attempted to live a good life, then you've obtained a great deal of spirituality, and your soul has indeed advanced tremendously. Even if you've fallen a few times, simply trying at all means that you've done better than you think.

The Eight Golden Keys are *fortitude, mercy, honesty or honor, loyalty, gratitude, psychic or healing ability, levity,* and *great or grand intelligence (infused knowledge).* And while it's true that everyone should abide by these concepts, they're mandatory for the mystical traveler.

### *The Golden Keys in Detail*

Let's go through each of the Keys, not only from a practical definition, but also from a spiritual point of view. In this way, you'll become more knowledgeable about the gifts they bring, along with the pitfalls you might encounter. Please note that even if you deviate from these Keys, it doesn't necessarily mean that you're off track. However, it does mean that you're not fulfilling your role as a mystical traveler.

## 1. Fortitude

The first Key may not be what you expect: It actually refers to steadfastness and endurance, even in the face of pain and illness (such as in the case of Montel Williams, who must continually fight his multiple sclerosis). If the soul is fortified, you'd be surprised by how the body follows. Examples of this abound in everyday life when strong-willed people live long, full lives even after doctors have given them a death sentence. Yet if the will isn't strong, the body will give up, causing someone to die—while they may not actually pass over to the Other Side, a life spark goes out and they become vacant and purposeless, like the walking dead. Drug addicts are very much in this category, as the fire of their souls has been smothered, and it's as if they aren't even in their physical shells anymore.

To be fortified also means to be strong in the face of all skepticism and adversity, and to bear witness to the truth. Mystical travelers can't be silent or quiet; they must be like Jesus and be strong enough to proclaim who they are and what they believe in. And, just as Christ did, they must spread the word about our all-loving Creators—but they can never shove their beliefs down others' throats or try to convert them against their will. It's important that they simply give answers to the questions they're asked and live by example.

Finally, this Key instructs mystical travelers to have constancy. The cry of "When is there time for me?!" must go away for advanced souls, as they're usually on call for anyone or any situation that needs them, and they'll be able to rest when they get Home. They are not "martyrs" to the cause, but are more like arrows that fly through all the dark days and nights, hitting the mark whenever they're required to help others and plant light columns of spirituality.

## 2. Mercy

The second Key is the plant from which the flowers of compassion and love bloom. Now, there are many types of love: We usually think about it as being between two romantic partners, which can be glorious, but it also spreads out to all kinds of people, places, beliefs, ideals, and purposes. In fact, the one love that sustains throughout eternity is that of God and self, followed by the love of others.

Mystical travelers must love Mother and Father God above all others; and with that love, everything else falls right into place. What you might not realize is that if you adore Them with your whole heart and soul, then that feeling will spill over to all of Their people and creatures. It's all right to look for love from others, because we *are* social and procreating entities, but without God it is all flat and meaningless.

It really bothers me when I hear people say, "I'll die if I don't get so-and-so." This kind of sentiment is so selfish, as no one should encumber another's heart to the point that he or she rules out God. There are many "love niches" in the human heart—into which children, parents, significant others, and so forth are tucked—but God must be in the *whole* heart. So if you don't defer to our Creators and truly love yourself as being created by Them, you should definitely not take on the mantle of the mystical traveler.

Remember, you came into this life to give glory to God: You were made, and charted your life, for Them. You were created to be the way you are from many lifetimes, and you are unique because there is no other entity like you anywhere in the universe. You experience for Them, so your sense of self should glorify Them.

Again, if you cannot give everything to God, then you can't be a mystical traveler. While it's not easy, taking on the mantle certainly doesn't mean that you must refrain from having ambition or striving to have a nice car or home. No one wants you in sackcloth and ashes, and the only way you can truly be poor or destitute is if you don't have a complete and total love of your wonderful Parents.

When you become a mystical traveler, it may seem like you're giving so much up, but as you can see, you'll get so much more in return. You simply need the courage to release what you think you want and need. Let me stop here and assure you that your house, job, car, and family won't mysteriously disappear, but everything will take on a new meaning. It gets to the point where what you think you need and want somehow changes in complexion, and your outlook on life is altered dramatically.

☨

Mercy and compassion come into play with all of those who are less fortunate than we are, which comprises a good portion of the world. Many special-interest groups and charities spring from mercy, and mystical travelers are often in the middle of them. Countless individuals *feel* mercy, but they don't act on it . . . whereas, advanced souls do. They tend to those who need help, including the homeless and indigent, and they feel tremendous empathy while doing so.

The only thing you have to be careful of here is not getting caught in the snares of people who can't be helped, for they become like parasites who feed off of you emotionally, mentally, or even financially. This is enabling others to use you, which means that you're not helping them at all. But it's wonderful to work with the elderly or youth organizations, start a charity, or just contribute to a nonprofit organization that you truly believe in.

You can also sponsor a little boy or girl from the Christian Children's Fund, which I've done. My sponsored child is now ten and goes to school, and she writes me about her progress and sends me pictures. Her English is strained, but it gets better with each letter, and all we hold dear in this life. We can't play anyone each other, and when we say we're going to do something,

tual people tend to stick by their word, no matter what. ple, Montel Williams and I have never had a contract in 7 years . . . it was by word alone that I agreed to be on w. It used to be that business arrangements were routinely is way, with a commitment and a handshake, and that . It's a sad commentary on our very litigious society that ren't done this way anymore.

u encounter people who don't stick by their word, then 't count on them. Yet you must still go on (albeit reluc- even though your trust in those folks has gone out the . Of course disloyalty hurts, but it should never deter you ur own word and beliefs.

nises and oaths come from loyalty to other people, as well uses, beliefs, and even your own soul's spirituality. Inner s extremely important, as you must be true to your per- ews and principles and not just go along with what the mode is. As William Shakespeare wrote: "To thine own rue." This internal process first starts with the belief of within your soul—this is when you truly understand the ity of who you are. You know you're determined to live e ability to be real and forthright in your beliefs, and noth- deter you.

main thing to remember here is that when you're loyal elf, you won't create a "warp." A warp occurs when you disloyal to yourself and go against the truth as you know ample, let's say that you become a member of a gang that rible things to others. Although you don't believe in hurt- one, out of loyalty to your gang you participate in their s and end up killing another person. This is an aberration personal truth, for you're being disloyal to yourself. No uld tell you what to do, especially when it's wrong.

must adhere to your own spiritual principles, and then go out and support others with your solid beliefs intact.

---

and I love to write her back. It really does only cost pennies a day, and how it makes me feel is indescribable. It's interesting that this young lady has the same birthday (February 19) as my psychic son, Chris; and the child he sponsors happens to be named Sylvia. So, even in the smallest incidents, you can see that there are no accidents.

### 3. Honesty or Honor

The third Key is *honesty or honor.* Honor governs actions and speech, mostly pertaining to treating others in a respectful way. Each person is part of God, so he or she deserves to be honored; that is, don't assume that a king's soul is more advanced than that of a beggar on the street.

In addition, it's important to honor your country and give it the due it is owed. When it comes to the USA, for instance, too many people have died to keep our way of life intact. The United States isn't always right in its actions, but its basic principles of freedom have allowed so many to bask in its greatness. And keep in mind that *all* governments have flaws because they're made up of imperfect human beings.

Honor also goes deep into the soul—you need to value who you are and where you came from, and especially show respect to the Creators Who made you. You should honor your physical self because it's the temple that houses your soul, so refrain from overindulgence and abusing it with substances that can ruin your health. As you were made in the image and likeness of God, when you get to the Other Side, you'll have a glorified body that glows with the fact that you've given honor to Them and yourself.

⁜

When it comes to honesty, this can be tougher than it sounds, as sometimes it must be separated from decorum or tact. Of course you shouldn't lie, be covert, or engage in any criminal activity—there is a universal honesty, which is always present in action, word, and deed. So when a woman asks you if she looks fat, rather than just saying yes, it's better to be kind and tactful.

Try something along the lines of, "Well, that dress pattern you're wearing isn't as flattering as some of the other items I've seen you in. Plus, I know how you feel—I've been bloated recently and am thinking of cutting back on sweets." Now, you've formed a partnership with the other person by using tact and including yourself . . . and you still didn't lie.

What if someone calls and you tell whoever answers the phone to say that you're not there? That just means what you've said: You're not there for that individual. This isn't cheating; you genuinely don't feel like dealing with this individual at the moment. Strangely enough, the person who advised me about this was a Catholic priest I knew when I was in college (not that I thought he was God's only authority); and the more I thought about it, the more truthful I felt it was. This is basically the same thing as when you don't answer the telephone because your caller ID indicates that it's someone you don't wish to talk to or cannot identify.

If kindness comes into play, you'll always be betting on a winner; and if you stand by your beliefs, you won't be deceived. Righteousness and truth can be sisters to each other, but false righteousness is never truth. So if you're aware of lies and dishonesty, you should expose them for the greater good rather than for the intent of vengeance or to make yourself seem more important. The universal truth that governs all of us means that you must be kind, caring, patient, and trustworthy. If you're true to yourself and your own spiritual principles, you'll never have to worry, as everyone who does good in truth is right.

However, as strange as this may sound, keep in mind that your truth may not be someone else's. You can see this particularly in different faiths and philosophies, which is one reason why I've always said, "Take with you what you want and leave the rest behind." I'd never write or speak anything untruthful to anyone, and I believe to the depths of my soul that everything I put out is true.

Having said that, I also realize
against established religions and beli
centuries. I'd rather have someone
write and say than not at all, and I
Instead, I rely on the truthfulness, log
to the world, and I allow people to co
More often than not, when people
embrace my teachings wholehearted
For those who can't always accept v
they'll at least embrace some of my i
their own realization, using what I'\
ment of their souls.

Honesty also keeps you from spre
what is someone else's truth is not n
you've heard is true, why do you ne
up a Pandora's box of hurt for anothe
seem to thrive on scandal, but are y
tant? Remember, whatever you put o
come back to you.

I also love what another priest t
good for one person, and that's you.
done in the past—as long as it didn
business and doesn't necessarily nee
people will confess portions of thei
proud of to current loved ones, and
very badly and are never forgotten b

You're not being deceitful if you
could potentially hurt a loving relatio
pened earlier in your life and would b
one you love in confessing it. Give it
guilt by just trying to be the best poss

### 4. Loyalt

This Key is my personal favorite
tion, simply means that we stick by o

friends,
against
we do it

Spir
For exai
almost
his shov
made tl
was tha
things

If y
you can
tantly)
window
from yo

Pro
as to ca
loyalty
sonal v
popular
self be
loyalty
comple;
up to th
ing can

The
to yours
become
it. For e
does te
ing any
activitie
of your
one sho

You
you can

Cast away any and all individuals who would make you betray yourself and what you believe in.

## 5. Gratitude

Gratitude is the fifth Golden Key of Knowledge. I know that there have probably been times when you've wondered, *What do I have to be grateful for? To come into this life and go through this hell?* And even when the glass of life is half full, you can still feel empty. Yet this is such a dismal way to live—no matter what condition you're in, there's something to be grateful for, even if you don't see it now. As macabre as this may sound, even if you're dying, being grateful that your pain is coming to an end and you're going Home is something worthwhile.

Health and prosperity are really what most of us need to be thankful for, especially in today's world, but it's not corny to say that we're also grateful for blue skies, rainbows, and autumn leaves; for our loved ones; for our jobs; and for the roofs over our heads. I remember when I was working for the homeless in Los Angeles and I got to talking to this woman who had come in for food. She mentioned how grateful she was for the good meal, but also for the fact that she was free and got to breathe fresh air. Now *that's* thankfulness we'd never suspect.

Many years later, I had the chance to speak to a 70-year-old lady who had buried four sons and a husband. Yet instead of just giving up and going crazy, she'd joined an order of Carmelite nuns who helped out prisoners and taught children. She told me, "I was so mad at God, and then I realized how grateful I was to experience this—so I could give hope and joy and explain my life to others, to help them through their trials." That's what I call true gratitude.

I don't mean to imply that we have to be meek and humble; rather, we should be strong and thankful. (Besides, our Parents don't mind if we get mad—They understand all human behavior and love all of us despite our foibles.) We must feel blessed that we're able to come down here to advance our souls and gain higher knowledge and spirituality. There is a quote from Francine that I love, which sums it all up: "I am grateful to be in this life to learn."

So take the time to appreciate your family members, a beautiful day, or the scent of flowers. If you condition yourself, the simplest things can make you happy. Just get rid of all the "what-ifs" of life—to live for the day, or even the hour, is so important. We've become a generation conditioned to negativity, one that's forgotten the joy of fresh-baked bread or a car that runs.

Don't get me wrong . . . we all love nice things. It's when the desire for them goes above and beyond what we need or could ever use that greed has wrapped its tentacles around us, and that awful word *entitlement* comes in. To be ungrateful or feel that we're entitled to anything at all is really the wrong road to embark upon. Believing that anything is owed to us is a deadly karmic trap. Tragically, we're living in a society full of individuals who feel that the world owes them . . . and it doesn't.

We see so much glutting of "stuff"—particularly during the holidays—that it's no wonder gratitude has taken a backseat. We're so inundated that our senses get overloaded; nothing is enough, and we start looking around to find what we can acquire to fill the gaping hole in our souls. (If you sit down and make a list of what you really need and compare it to a list of what you aspire for, you'll become alarmed.) Simplification is much easier than filling our lives with things we feel we can't live without. And usually after we *do* get these things, we're *still* not happy. In fact, people are afraid to say that they're happy for fear that God will hear and rain destruction on them, which is a sad and untrue superstition.

Be thankful for all the large and small joys in life, and plow through the bad times to advance your soul. The old caring song "The Best Things in Life Are Free" is not too far from the truth, so be glad that you have another day to do good and glorify God. To live by this example will be like a beam of light in a darkened world.

## 6. Psychic or Healing Ability

The sixth Key is *psychic or healing ability*. Certainly not all psychics or healers are mystical travelers—many are charlatans, and others are what we might call "pseudo psychics" who don't have much ability and are mainly in it for ego or glorification of self. However, all advanced souls always have these gifts to some degree, although they may not become famous for them. Different mystical travelers will take on different roles; and while some may prefer to do God's work in basic anonymity, others who do it on a larger scale usually gain some type of fame as a natural by-product. (A great example of this would be the late Edgar Cayce.)

Psychic or healing ability can reside and manifest in almost anyone, but it's almost always accentuated in mystical travelers and helps them in their work. They have a great sense of discernment, not only when it comes to other people, but in different situations as well. Thus, they're often allowed to help others with their illnesses, without them even realizing it.

For years, so many people, churches, and even societies tried to separate spirituality from the psychic realm, which is incredibly wrong and unreasonable. The more we reach up and question, the more we're able to see ahead and sense dark from light and right from wrong . . . and from there, it gets more advanced. We all have the power to see and feel angels, hear our guides, and even feel or see our Creators. The tragedy is that we've been told for hundreds of years that we couldn't, as the ability was only for the select few, who were usually religious leaders or so-called prophets.

People think it's just too simplistic to ask for psychic ability, which is ridiculous, since we were all born with it. We constantly see this in children . . . that is, until life beats it out of them. You may have noticed an increasing number of men and women on television telling me the amazing things their children do, such as calling out the names of passed-over loved ones whom they never knew, or relating stories about past lives that can be validated.

A classic example was when I was on *Montel* and this woman reported that her preschool-aged daughter told her about living in Mexico, even though their family had no lineage or ties to that country or anywhere else in Latin America. The child talked about things that the mother had to look up and confirm, and when they were at a zoo and the little girl identified a rabbit indigenous to Mexico, a man overheard and asked how she could possibly know that. This woman told me that her daughter even watches Spanish shows on TV and seems to understand what's being said. She must, or why would she sit there and watch them?

And just as we all possess psychic ability, so too can we heal. As with anything, some people will be better at it than others because their kinetic or electrical energy is stronger—but *anyone* who gives him- or herself up to be a tube by which God's energy comes through can be a healer. The person is only replacing some of his or her energy with God's in doing so. (Please note that there's quite a bit more information on healing in Chapter 7.)

## 7. Levity

You may find this Key to be out of place at first, but when you look deeper, you'll see how important it is to life and well-being. Think about it for a second: Do you know of anyone who is truly loved who doesn't have at least a decent sense of humor? One who can not only make others laugh but can also poke fun at him- or herself? It is levity that keeps negativity away—it's a way to look on the bright side, to be positive, and to find joy in adversity.

Of course I'm not belittling grief and the tough times of life, but if you can't find something positive in your world, you're doomed for depression. I don't need to tell you that there have been studies in which even terminally ill people got better after watching funny movies or experiencing humorous situations. It turns out that laughter actually sends an endorphin through the body that heals.

Humor is one of the greatest gifts our Parents have given us. We may be deeply upset or sad, but then we watch entertainers such as Robin Williams, Bill Cosby, or the late Dean Martin (who had a great sense of humor but was more known for his singing ability), and it suddenly lifts up our spirits. Even troubles can be humorous, and those who recognize that fact are generally much happier than the average human being is. Mystical travelers usually have a great sense of humor and laugh a lot, knowing that it boosts the spirits of those around them and brings about a more positive atmosphere in which to do God's work.

Years ago when I was in college, there was a nun who told me that I'd always make it through life because I had a sense of humor. Sometimes things get so bad that our only choice is to laugh. And if we try, we can see humor in anything. For example, I watch my dogs and laugh at some of their antics, and my grandchildren really crack me up. Kids are so honest and guileless when they're younger, and the little tidbits of truth and wisdom that they put out often hit the mark, especially when they inadvertently target an unsuspecting adult.

You should be aware that joy comes from inside and never outside, but to be with friends and family and laugh is the greatest gift. To make others happy and provide some levity gives joy and energy back to you—but it's even more important to be able to laugh at yourself. Never take yourself that seriously because change is always occurring and life doesn't stand still . . . so why not have some laughs in the process?

## 8. Great or Grand Intelligence (Infused Knowledge)

The eighth Golden Key is what we call the "bonus" Key, since it really encompasses the other seven. With great intelligence also comes infused knowledge, which increases our ability to understand and have greater inductive and deductive reasoning. Infused knowledge not only elevates our desire to learn and explore, but it's also a great motivator for higher spirituality. And it isn't just the spiritual side of things that we begin to understand—*everything* in our chart (and others') becomes clear to us. We really start to feel that we've been looking through pea-soup fog until now, and the more the mantle of the mystical traveler settles upon us, the clearer our vision becomes.

Many times this infused knowledge comes to us in the form of either direct or indirect communication from God, our spirit guides, or our angels. We may be in the middle of something that's a big key to our success, when we suddenly just "know" how to handle it. It's one of God's ways of communicating, as well as being an effective tool for the Other Side.

You see, whenever someone over there wants an invention or a cure to manifest, they simply implant the idea in one of us here on Earth, who can then take that idea and make it come to fruition. The ideas that come to us are amazing; what's even more interesting is that the ability to express ourselves on paper or with word and deed gets better, as we learn (or, I should say, "are more infused with") great diplomacy and tact.

Please understand that intelligence doesn't just come from books. Yes, I've found that being an avid reader has helped me in reference work, but even if you don't read that much, knowledge will come to you. And as it seems that the need to learn and explore becomes overwhelming, you might actually find yourself reading more. It's almost as if you feel that there's so much to take in and not enough time to do so. Also, when you get Home, you'll keep on researching and learning for God, so you can realize all kinds of different facets in order to become more advanced. You'll see your fellow mystical travelers in medicine, science, writing, and any field that helps people make their lives better in any way.

### Keeping on Track

As someone who's on a spiritual path, you'll find it helpful to do a mental checklist of the Keys morning and night. Ask to be kept on track, and then name all Eight Keys for yourself and all those around you. Yes, you'll be talking to God, but more important, you'll be communicating with the divinity inside of you. Don't let yourself get wobbly because of the bombardment of so much darkness that's around you. Think of yourself with true esteem and remember that you're full of knowledge.

Before you know it, you'll be able to heal and become a light column that pushes away darkness. You'll discover that when you give your will to God, everything in life becomes better and you're able to endure. It's very much like when Moses was in the desert and manna fell from heaven—but in this case, you'll be getting the grace and strength to fight the battle against evil. If you keep repeating the Keys, this brings power in and of itself. Even if you don't want to become a mystical traveler, the practice will still lift your soul and make you stronger and more advanced.

Francine states that the more spiritual one becomes, the more questions such as "Am I doing the right thing?" or "Am I on track?" arise. She says, "A person who is not spiritual never asks these questions. Sylvia always says that when someone wonders how they're doing spiritually, she never worries about them. A person who isn't spiritual doesn't care and certainly never asks."

The biblical question of "For what shall it profit a man, if he shall gain the whole world, and lose his own soul? (Mark 8:36)" is very apt for those who don't have spirituality or follow the Eight Golden Keys of Knowledge. As a mystical traveler you can never, ever compromise your belief system for some external reason. There is no such thing as sin, but this *is* a blight against your own soul.

As a mystical traveler, you must give your will entirely to God without question or withdrawal. This leads to constant evaluation of self to make sure that you're doing everything for your Parents, and that's where the Golden Keys can really help. Even if you don't want to become a mystical traveler, it won't hurt to keep yourself audited and evaluated spiritually.

It's best to put a list of the Keys in big bold type in a prominent place where you can see them every day. Even now as you're reading this book, mentally check yourself. You know yourself better than anyone else, so you'll know if you're an honest person. (As an aside, the saying "honest to a fault" has always baffled me, since how could honesty ever be a fault?) You'll also know where you've failed at certain points.

Sometimes to fail is good if you realize it, pick yourself up and right yourself, and never do it again. You cannot lose what you believe in or compromise—not even for the pleasure of the moment. Physical pleasure is part of life and wonderful, but not when it's at the expense of others or yourself. Always remember the old adage about being kind to all the people you meet on your way up because you'll meet them again on the way down.

When you put your Eight Golden Keys on paper, take out a calendar, too. If you did some good act during a particular day, put a star on that date. I know you may think that this is juvenile, like you're back in school getting gold stars, but this act imprints the good you've done on your mind . . . and if you didn't, then you can try harder the next day. Eventually you'll get to the point where you won't need to have a scorecard, so to speak. Some might prefer to have a diary or a journal to describe their days, which is fine, but do try to perform a good deed every day. You can bolster yourself up to do so by continually saying to yourself, "I'm doing this for You, God."

There's so much time that we waste watching mindless television programs or just sitting and daydreaming when we could be doing something productive. Of course the other night I enjoyed dinner with friends and then came home and did some needlepointing rather than writing. Yet I felt no guilt because earlier I'd spoken to two police officers about a case and did some readings.

I also understand in my bones that there's essentially a ninth Golden Key, and that's *commitment*. If you're not committed, all the rest falls short. So, what if you want to live by the Keys but don't wish to take the unconditional oath, give up your will, and go anywhere God orders? That's absolutely fine. However, I guarantee that if you start living by the Keys, your spirituality will have grown so much, and your love of God will have increased so much, that you'll just automatically want to become a mystical traveler.

✟

Pride has always been looked upon as a negative and self-serving emotion: We say things like "You're prideful," or "You're awfully full of pride." And have you ever wondered why the Catholic Church was so against pride? Well, it's because they wanted to knock people down and make them subservient to their rule, yet their hierarchy was the epitome of pridefulness.

Like any emotion or deed, pride can indeed be taken too far. Now there's nothing wrong with taking pride in yourself, your accomplishments, and how you've overcome adversity. Being proud of your children, your good actions, your country, or passing a very difficult test are also fine. It's when pride becomes a manifestation of an overblown ego that it becomes negative. We've all seen the type of person who's so full of himself that he can't see the forest for the trees.

Yet we must also guard against false humility. After all, the Revolutionary War would never have taken place if the early Americans had just given up. One of my favorite flags from that era is the one that warns: DON'T TREAD ON ME, and that succinctly sums up the concept of false humility. The United States' forefathers wouldn't have come here to find freedom if they were lacking in courage, as well as dignity and *true* humility. When British rule became too oppressive, they revolted and won freedom. To this day, America is still the most free of all the nations on this planet—and it certainly wasn't won by humble people who stood back and bowed down to oppression. It was more a case of "I'm proud of my life, my people, and my beliefs; and I will fight for them."

As Francine says, "Righteous men and women audit themselves sometimes daily, but without guilt. Please get over false humility . . . it's really a flaw in your human nature to let people walk all over you in the name of 'being humble.' Stand tall if you're spiritual or a mission-life entity, and especially if you've taken on the mantle of mystical traveler."

If you simply can't live by the Eight Keys with your whole heart and soul, then you'll probably never be a mystical traveler, but you can still be a very advanced soul. If you've tried your best (and that's all that God expects), then you should hold your head high. Always try to carry yourself with honor, truth, love, gratitude, and a righteous type of pride. In fact, every white entity should take pride in what he or she has learned.

Remember that if you don't choose to be a mystical traveler, there's no shame or retribution—as a mission-life entity, you'll also live a life dedicated to God. But for those of you who will become mystical travelers, it's perfectly okay to be proud of your spiritual accomplishment. Even if you had to petition long and hard to be a part of this mission of life, you and your chart were accepted for the challenge. The Bible says that many are called but few are chosen, but I feel that many are called but few complete their missions. Of course you and you alone are the only one who can give up your will and choose, so never diminish yourself because you carry the royal mantle of God's embassy.

✢ ✢ ✢

# Chapter Seven

# EFFECTS OF THE ASCENT IN SPIRITUALITY

Although you'll have to endure a lot of hardship as an advanced entity, there are many "perks" that will help you out. For example, being a mystical traveler aids you in balancing your intellect (which is the genetic part of Father God) with your emotion (which is the genetic part of Mother God). When you have too little emotion, you become a borderline personality—almost as if you have to attach to another person to fulfill that side of you that doesn't love, feel, or create. This doesn't mean that you're consciously negating Azna, but psychologists do state that a borderline personality comes from the unapproachable mother.

I feel that this condition can be courtesy of a human mother, but it's also because one had negated the side of him- or herself that can accept beauty or those things that are there but unseen. For such an individual, everything must be approached with analytic perfection, and nothing is real unless proven. Of course we can have too much emotion and, again, miss the beauty around us. Emotion is wonderful, but too much of it overflows on the intellect and makes us frantic and worried because there is no logical control.

Luckily, mystical travelers have been given a greater ability to cement the intellect and emotion, and they may become very psychic and have the power to astral-travel as well. They'll find themselves becoming great healers, too—the ability comes rapidly, and they'll be able to use it both mentally and physically.

### The Healing Process

Anyone can heal, but advanced souls often do it with more strength than others do, and they can even see faster results. Yet if you're not a mystical traveler, I don't want to discourage you from healing because you *can* absolutely do a transfer of energy.

Make sure you begin by surrounding yourself and the person you're healing with white light, and then thread green light through his or her body. Next, you can follow the very simple process that the ministers of Novus Spiritus do after every service. They wait until after the service is over and stand behind those who want healing, who are seated. If the minister is female, she simply puts her right hand on top of the person's head, and then places her left hand over that. If it's a male minister, the hands are reversed—his left hand would be on top of the individual's head, and his right hand would go over that.

This signifies and recognizes the left and right sides of the brain, and how they typically work with the sexes: Males generally operate from the left sides of their brains, while females tend to be dominated by the right sides of their brains. However, this can be individually different, so you might want to experiment to see which hand placement works better for you.

After the placement of hands, all ministers surround both themselves and the people being healed with the white light of the Holy Spirit, and then they ask that they become tubes by which God's energy flows through to heal those who need it and can benefit from that energy. It's as simple as that, and very effective. Our ministers have had great success in healings, and men and women invariably stand up in our churches to relate that they feel 100 percent better.

You don't have to pay for lessons in healing unless you're going to become a doctor, an acupuncturist, a hypnotherapist, or the like. It's always baffling to me when people who do holistic or faith healing follow rituals or ritualistic practices and overcomplicate it. Our Parents know what we need—we're all Their children and have the power to channel Their energy. Thus, we don't have to explain ourselves and what we're doing to Them.

Healers don't even have to necessarily know where an illness is, for they're just the vehicles that Mother and Father God's grace and healing energy comes through, with no effect on them. There's no ego involved, for They are the Ones doing the healing. Everyone can do this, although it's true that some may be better at it than others. However, the more you do it, the better you'll get at it, whether you're a mystical traveler or not.

### Climbing the Golden Ladder

As you progress more as a mystical traveler, your sensitivity will increase, but you'll become impervious to much of the negativity others feel. If someone berates you, you won't seem to mind, or it won't hurt you like it would have before. With all the hard work you do for yourself and God, you'll receive definite benefits as well. God never takes without giving . . . not just in like measure, but a hundredfold. That's why when you do acts such as giving seed money to a worthy cause, it comes back to you again and again.

You'll be able to discern dark from light more than most people, thanks to your increased sensitivity. Your innate psychic ability will become heightened; and you'll become more insulated from things that had a tendency to bother, hurt, or worry you. It's almost like your antennae (for lack of a better word) are being pulled out and are reaching more toward God, instead of being so concerned with all the worries of the Earth plane.

I think this fits perfectly with what Francine said so many years ago, which took me years to understand: "Be above the body, not in it." You become far more aware of actions and body language, which those in the scientific world call "neurologistics." You begin to detest lying and subversive actions—this may bother you for a while, but it's better than living life in the dark.

The more you climb what we might call "the golden ladder to God," the better you can deal with life and survive. This doesn't mean that you're immune from bad things happening, however. For example, when my last husband ran off with another woman, he claimed it was because I was too popular. The fact that he was my business manager and booked me into everything evidently didn't figure into his reasoning about my popularity. While I felt great pain, no one could believe how well I recovered and went on with my life . . . which I owe to taking on the mantle of the mystical traveler.

If you decide to become a mystical traveler, you'll find that certain people separate from you because they see that you've changed; that is, they pick up on the brilliant light that emanates from you. They're not necessarily bad or dark-souled entities (although you will be rid of such individuals), but they won't be able to understand your light and may even fear it. While you may find that some friends and family members drop away from you or become more distant, it won't be because of anything you've done. Many times they'll be afraid that they're losing you, which couldn't be further from the truth. It's just that once you've found the ladder to God, there really isn't anything stronger than that.

Please don't feel bad, for it's just as well. These men and women are simply not spiritually advanced enough yet to accept your evolution. Conversely, those who are pursuing their own progression—which isn't just limited to other mystical travelers—will gravitate toward you almost immediately.

As you make the ascent in spirituality, it will affect every aspect of your life; but you'll find that any envy, deception, and hurt directed your way will be beneath you. You'll hit the next rung on the ladder with the understanding that all people incur their own karma—this is just the rule, and you'll rise above it. You'll also stop being so hard on yourself, as your soul begins to expand and magnify Jesus and our Creators.

It is said that wisdom comes from listening to what the heart and soul already know; when *your* heart and soul know the truth, they come to rest on the fact that you're doing or believing in what's right for you. The more you know, the brighter your soul becomes—but many won't have your knowledge and evolvement, so it can be a lonely existence. Yet if you have patience, you'll find those who are like you.

However, I'd like to put to rest the fear that if you become a mystical traveler, you'll absolutely become separated from the ones you love because you're an advanced soul and they're not. Francine says that silent knowledge sometimes goes out to family and friends that makes them realize they're just like us. Taking on the mantle doesn't mean that you'll be prevented from spending time with your loved ones both in life and on the Other Side. In fact, when mystical travelers die and return Home, they often find that their entire families have taken on the mantle, too.

Again, advanced souls don't only hang around each other in little groups or cliques, and they don't have extra halos or any distinguishing marks—the mantle is invisible except to other mystical travelers. So if you're not an advanced entity but your spouse is, it won't in any way affect your love for, or devotion to, each other. It would be no different if he or she were the president of a large company and you were a salesperson. Would that mean you didn't love each other or stick together? Of course not. Don't start thinking that your human knowledge is privy to the Divine plan of our Creators.

⸸

Mystical travelers do suffer in life because their senses get keener, so they see things in sharper focus than others do. The injustices, the cruelty, and so forth cause great discomfort because they can't serve everyone or do everything. As time goes on, though, they come to the realization that they can only do what's possible in their own circle of life—otherwise it would drive them crazy. You'll find them fighting for animal rights, the homeless, the environment, and health care; as well as donating time and money to children, the elderly, and the sick. Even if they just counsel and help people, that in itself is a great challenge.

So, when you accept the mantle, your sensitivity gets deeper and more acute; but to counteract that, your strength and ability to cope increase. It is at times bittersweet. You're not going to take on being a mystical traveler and then suddenly be hurt more than you've ever been before . . . no, you're actually more insulated from pain. You begin to see everything for what it truly is and don't bring your own hurts or memories with it. It's like the scales fall away from your eyes, and you're not as empathetic anymore. Of course the sympathy is there, but once you get plugged in with too much empathy, you become useless. I know that if I hadn't been somewhat objective over the years, I wouldn't have been much use to anyone.

As a mystical traveler, you have to force yourself to concentrate on the wonders of life and be positive. After some practice, you'll learn to live in the *now*. The nagging sense of *I should have done this* or *I didn't do that* is slowly taken away. Such worries are really deterrents because they can cause guilt and keep you from what you can do right now and in the future. Yesterday is gone; while tomorrow is a new start to heal, help, and elevate your spirituality.

If you get caught up in the suffering of life rather than knowing it's for your soul's perfection, you can become bogged down and not live up to your mission. This is probably the hardest test because your senses are so heightened that you see and feel everything more deeply than others do. But you can turn this into a blessing because the deeper the feelings become, the more understanding comes, too.

You approach every entanglement with objectivity, infused knowledge, and caring—but not to the point that you can't function or are unable to help. After all, if you're in the trenches and a fellow soldier and you are both wounded, you have to tend to yourself before you can help the other person or you'll both die.

The other facet that advanced souls tend to conquer more quickly is "cell memory." While most of us can carry over past-life fears and phobias, once the mantle drops, it seems to also cleanse the soul of those fears and phobias. Some memory of them will still exist, but it becomes distant and neutralized in the cells. Again, with hardship comes many blessings.

That's why Francine says that more than other entities, mystical travelers adjust faster. Of course they're not perfect, but they certainly do have an extra passion and fire in their bellies. They also usually "die on their feet," so to speak—they don't retire from their duties, but instead keep on until they leave this planet. Another blessing is that they seem to go Home very quickly. Many of my ministers are mystical travelers, and the four who have died did go quite fast and were even found with their arms crossed.

### The Neutralizers of Negative Energy

I often hold salons, in which 40 to 50 people spend the day with me. It's very intimate and gratifying because we can talk about more advanced theology, exchange ideas, and ask questions. One of the things I always stress in these salons is: "Never be so quick to judge others." I explain that when it comes to the individuals I don't particularly like, that's my thing, not theirs. Sometimes it's true that what we don't like in others is a reflection of what we don't like in ourselves.

When the mantle drops, it also gives people more courage to stand up for what's right. It's not that mystical travelers have to cause disturbances, but they certainly have no fear when it comes to speaking out against injustice. It's much like Jesus taking the whip to the money changers in the temple—even though he wasn't an avid attendee at that temple, he saw a wrong that needed to be righted. As full of love, compassion, and truth as he was, Jesus had no problem fighting for righteousness.

Keepers of justice don't have to be popes or preachers—they just have to lead exemplary lives full of grace and assistance.

They must also remember that it's easier for some people to let things run their course. This doesn't mean that such individuals are cowards; it just means that they haven't taken on being soldiers for God.

It is imperative that all mystical travelers conquer impatience (which may not be an easy task because they're activists and doers), and they must guard against being overzealous. They can audit their thoughts and actions, but not to the point that they develop a scrupulous consciousness. You see, if they became afraid of every word or thought they had, that would deflect all the goodness and joy that came to them. Rather, these advanced souls simply have to live the best they can by the rules and let the rest go. And by "the rules," I mean the ones that decree that human beings should be given back their own souls' control, rather than being taken control of.

Due to also being infused with precognitive and other psychic abilities, mystical travelers soon find themselves being peacemakers and seeing the truth in all situations. They'll also develop telepathy—while every person's prayers are important, these advanced souls will find that they have a knack for making things come true. Consider Christ: Sure he suffered, but look at how he healed and helped and allowed people to see a perfect, loving God. We can all do this, but it's the mystical travelers' calling . . . a lifelong career.

✤

One of the boons to taking the oath is that advanced souls can overcome everyday problems more rapidly than others do. Let's use illness as an example.

While it might take years to heal from an illness or disease, mystical travelers have the ability to shorten the process. Of course advanced souls still have their life charts, and illness may factor in to them, but many times they can tweak their charts to better slide through the adversities of life. They know that their learning process is greater, so they're able to function above these obstacles.

Mystical travelers don't automatically receive the cures for life's maladies, but they *are* imbued with great endurance. (Look at Montel Williams: Yes, he suffers from MS, but it never keeps him from traveling and doing good works.) Indeed, many mystical travelers have very painful illnesses, but the one thing I've seen is that they handle them better and tend to get over them faster than other people do. These entities' suffering seems to be more of a mental one from continually trying to make the world better and relieve its injustices . . . or at least alleviate the pain of family and friends. But they will find themselves enjoying better health than most. They'll also feel that they're living in a youthful timelessness, no matter what their chronological age may be.

As a mystical traveler, you'll have the power to almost merge with people on this side. It's not like the Other Side, where you can actually go *into* another person; rather, you can be in the presence of others and seemingly absorb their thoughts and fears. Even if you don't tell them that you're a mystical traveler, they'll just feel better in your presence. People will migrate toward you, and if you're in a social situation such as a party, you'll find that you quickly have a crowd around you.

You'll also be able to leave behind an aftermath of your aura's residue. Even though you're in full force as a neutralizer of negative energy, once you leave a situation or place, part of your essence will be left there. It's as if you've left a light column of your aura behind for the benefit of others. Other people feel comfort when they're around you, almost like a type of security they can't put their finger on. They'll ask, "What's so different about you?" or "What have you been doing to yourself?" Or they'll remark, "You seem so bright."

The worst thing you can do is feel that you're better or more special or holy than anyone else. You never hear that Jesus strutted around—he was a plain and unpretentious teacher, as were Buddha and Mohammed. Giving up your will is a very humbling gift from

God that you accept with gratitude, commitment, loyalty, and the fervor to help other people with no thought of self.

You can live well, but not at the expense of others by lying and cheating and stepping on them to gain material wealth, fame, or power. If you go through life with goodness, love, truth, and honor, then the rewards of the world will find you. When you get "in the groove," such gracious behavior becomes second nature to you.

### Taking It Up a Notch

Now you may be asking, "Can mystical travelers ever live normally?" Sure, they can. They can have families, homes, good jobs, and fun . . . but what's always in the front of their awareness is their drive to make life better for others.

I'm convinced that all white entities live good lives, even though they can fall, but mystical travelers take it up another notch. They're truly the ones who typify what Cyrano de Bergerac meant when he said that he wanted to go to God with his white plume intact. He didn't want the feather he always wore on his hat to be sullied, which symbolized that he'd never compromised his morals for his own gain.

Let's face it, this planet really is a battleground between good and evil like no other. The old hymn "Onward, Christian Soldiers" is not so corny or far-fetched when the good go to battle the evil. When I was younger and used to sing that hymn in the Episcopalian church (I also grew up with the Catholic, Lutheran, and Jewish religions), I used to wonder who we were going off to fight against. As I got older and listened to my psychic grandmother and Francine, I began to realize just how unfeeling so many people were, as well as how many atrocities there were in this world . . . and I don't mean to be pessimistic, but it's getting worse. My spirit guide says that no other planet has as much war, pestilence, infamy, political corruption, unrest, and crime as we do. So why do we come here?

Before I incarnated this time, I asked my guide whether it would be difficult. She replied, "Yes, but not as difficult as you might think. Even if some people don't get what you're saying, you certainly won't be killed and tortured like those in the Dark Ages were who didn't believe in the way those in authority wanted wanted them to. As you know, first people were killed for being Christian, and then later on they were burned at the stake and tortured during the Inquisition for being heretical. This will not happen to you." This gave me great comfort . . . not that I'm a chicken.

Francine and Raheim say that this planet still needs spiritual awakening. God knows we humans were aware of what Earth was about before we incarnated, but after many lives of perfecting, it would be frightening to know that there was someplace else as horrific as this is. So thankfully, if we're called on to go to another world, we won't have to suffer like we do here.

Even when we go to other planets, we can always come back to "home base," as it were. I think that after many lives, we feel beat-up and tired, which is why we stay on our own Other Side and visit with our loved ones. However, we have the option to incarnate again, or we can be a protector or spirit guide who infuses the simplistic knowledge I'm putting forth in this book.

All entities can visit any and all of the planets and bring back information; they can see how they live, what their beliefs are, or what their way of life is—it's not just limited to mystical travelers. Some even choose to incarnate on one of these planets, but that's more the exception than the rule. I think that after they've been here for many lives, they're just too burned-out to go into life again, so they stay in our glorified Home, surrounded by joy and bliss. And as for me, although I might change my mind, for now I'd just as soon stay in spirit form. . . .

✣ ✣ ✣

# CHAPTER EIGHT

# SKEPTICS, DARK ENTITIES, AND OTHER CHALLENGES

It's true that mystical travelers put themselves out there more than anyone else because they're always bearing witness to their beliefs and trying to be examples of their spirituality. If they don't "practice what they preach," then they're not true mystical travelers.

This means that they have to wade through the marsh of what they don't like—whether it's people, places, or things—in order to get to the Other Side. In their advancement, they realize that all humans fall and make mistakes. I've certainly made them, and anyone who thinks that they haven't is living in an overblown bubble of self and ego.

Mystical travelers try to keep themselves above all that; if they do get caught in the mire, they pull themselves out very quickly. They don't stay there and wallow in the self-pity of how they've been wronged or put out, how nobody appreciates them, or how they've been maligned and are innocent. The bottom line is that they know the truth, as do our Creators, and that's all that matters.

All advanced entities spread the news about what Mother and Father God are really like, incorporating a philosophy that includes the belief in an afterlife and the Other Side, as well as fighting dogmas that instill guilt and fear. Unfortunately, in the process they're continually faced with negativity (and one of its biggest components, bigotry), and this does have an effect.

Since mystical travelers are only human, they're certainly not perfect—and even Jesus himself was known to doubt. Those who are channelers must take extra care to surround themselves with white light and prevent their own egos from getting in. If they start making things complicated or let their intellect take over, the ability will get gummed up. No one is able to keep his or her channels clear 100 percent of the time, as only God can do that. So when advanced souls' channels become clogged by an overabundance of negativity, their abilities can suffer, causing them to be wrong or make poor judgments.

Lawyers, doctors, accountants, and members of other professions can make a mistake and no one says anything . . . but let a psychic falter once, and all hell breaks loose. For example, there was this lost boy a while back who psychic medium James Van Praagh and I both thought was dead. James even went to Missouri and told the police where the child was killed—however, when he was found alive, it wasn't James who had to take the brunt of the criticism, it was me. Later I discovered that there were two other boys missing from the same area, and I believe we were picking up on one of them. Yet I was still reviled because I missed and was incorrect.

No one followed up on these other boys, and the skeptics and naysayers never seem to mention all the people I *have* saved or found. It seems that some folks just want to jump all over the fact that I've been wrong—whenever that happens, I've had to take stock of all the times I've been right and forget the rest. I find that I'm my own worst critic, but I also know in my heart and soul that I always have good intentions and the motive to help others in any way I can.

I'm telling you all of this so you can learn to thicken your own skin and realize that our Creators know where your intentions lie. No one with any real intelligence expects you to be 100 percent right as only They are, but you do have to be more right than wrong. This is what discourages people, however—they'll get 100 things right and then have 2 wrongs and give up altogether.

Nobody is perfect, and every single human being in history has failed. It's the same with healing—you won't be able to heal everyone all the time. I was talking to a medical intuitive the other day, and she was bemoaning the fact that she'd missed one patient's diagnosis. I responded, "But what about your successes? Why would you concentrate on one person when maybe it wasn't in her chart to be helped? Maybe it was written that she needed to go through this experience of illness for her own perfection." She did agree with me on that.

Here's a story that proves my point. Kathy was a minister in my church and had an advanced case of multiple sclerosis, which confined her to a wheelchair. Many asked her, "If you ministers are so good, why aren't you healed?" She replied, "But what you don't see is that I *am*. I know my soul is well and ready to meet God, and it never would have been before."

There are many ways to be healed apart from the body. The soul and mind can be healed with knowledge and belief, and since Kathy knew exactly where she was going, she was in fact cured. Instances such as these do keep you humble and more diligent.

This chapter will serve to illustrate that being a mystical traveler won't give you a free pass to escape ridicule, skepticism, hurt, and even defamation. Even so, those of you who know what's in your hearts will stay on course and continue to do your best. Those who aren't up for the battle this planet makes you face will fall, and that's all right. It takes great courage and steadfastness to be a mystical traveler, and not everyone can pick themselves up and go on. Again, no one person is better than any other in our Parents' eyes . . . They love us all equally, no matter what.

### Facing the Skeptics

Armed with their mantles, the Eight Golden Keys of Knowledge, and a total belief in a loving Mother and Father, mystical travelers go out into the world . . . and they must be prepared to fight negativity whenever and wherever they find it.

Speaking of which, I remember when I was on *Larry King Live* once with several skeptics, along with fellow mediums Char Margolis and James Van Praagh. A true skeptic tries to remain objective, but those who only want to debunk psychics should call themselves "anti-psychic"and let it go at that.

What amused me is how violent these particular individuals were, and that they had no other agenda than to put us down. I kept thinking, *Why are you yelling and screaming so, and why do we frighten you?* James and Char valiantly fought back, but I pretty much kept quiet because I knew we wouldn't be able to change them. I'm too old for this, and not just chronologically—I've been a medium so long and have too much information to get out to let this sort of thing bother me.

These so-called critics were so adamant about attacking our character, along with our beliefs about God, angels, the Other Side, and so forth . . . only to say that they didn't personally believe in God. Such is the case with professional skeptic/magician James Randi, which is perfectly all right. After all, if I pretended to let him believe whatever he wants but then turned around and put his beliefs and words down, I'd be a hypocrite. If James Randi and those like him choose to be atheists, that is their affair.

However, Mr. Randi and other anti-psychic skeptics have called me a liar and a charlatan numerous times, and there are even entire Websites devoted to trying to stop my work for God. How miserable is it that instead of helping others, some people choose to start atheistic or skeptical societies and ridicule, or even try to destroy, the men and women who *are* trying to help others?

As I keep saying, we must all be wary of those individuals who put themselves on a sick pedestal of occult practices (like a Jim Jones) or the hypocritical evangelicals (such as Jim Bakker and many others) who prey on fear and demand money and total obedience. It's so much better to disseminate truth and then let other people decide what they want. As I always say, take with you what you want and leave the rest behind.

✝

I often think that if it wasn't for those of us who are fighting to be mystical travelers and do good, many skeptics wouldn't have a purpose. Nevertheless, they can charge up to $25,000 for a membership in their organizations, for which you get a cup, a T-shirt, and a card saying that you're an atheist; as well as a personal meeting and dinner with the founder. What a deal! I only wish these skeptics would try to help other true psychics and me go after the people who use our names and erroneously bilk the public for thousands of dollars to remove curses. Even as I write these words, I'm working with the police to try to put some of these people in jail.

We mystical travelers are sitting ducks for those who will lie and do whatever they can to pull us down. I know this firsthand, but I also know that we can't give them power. No matter where we go, there they are, putting down everyone in the public eye—including Oprah, psychics, and the Pope—for the good works they do. They've even said I don't write my own books . . . well, thank God I keep my manuscripts on file, so my handwritten words can be compared against any of my published works. Yet even when you give them proof, such individuals won't ever admit they were wrong and retract their lies.

For a time these things hurt, but we must have the fortitude to go on. We all have to take the good with the bad and forge ahead. As I told psychic medium John Edward sometime ago when he was being blasted (and unfortunately still is): "Those who love you will always love you, and those who don't won't, so just let it go."

I have neither the time nor the inclination to waste my energies fighting those who are so vitriolic in their attacks on me and other legitimate mediums. Unfortunately, I know at least two younger psychics who are destroyed by every negative word they receive. When they call me to ask what to do, I always answer with the old saying about "sticks and stones." Then I invariably ask them if they truly believe in what they're doing.

Belief is a quiet, true philosophy that settles in your soul, so you don't have to defend yourself against it. No one will *ever* be able to shake my belief system and what I know to be true. If you're ingrained in your mission and faith like I am, you're not unlike the early Christians facing the lions; you must realize that you're not going to please everyone or have them agree with you.

I often wonder what purpose skeptics have in attacking belief systems. I know that we have freedom of speech, but to hit at the heart of faith and other people's way of life should be off-limits. I think that many atheists have over-the-top egos, but they should just do their thing and leave the rest of us alone. You'd think that they would embrace the motto of "live and let live," considering that their lack of belief in God puts them in the minority, but like agnostics (which are nothing more to me than watered-down atheists), their self-importance often rules their lives.

After that aforementioned show, Larry King told me, "Sylvia, you're a good sport," and I just smiled. I know that he was kindly trying to soften the blows he thought I'd taken, but I wanted to tell my dear friend that it would take a hell of a lot more than several skeptics who admitted that they'd never read one of my books to get me down. I can't ever win in that type of situation, and guess what? I don't even want to play. That's because my belief of helping and loving others isn't a game.

### Understanding Dark Entities

While skeptics can be very annoying, they're not necessarily dark souls, or those individuals who exude negativity and chaos and are the antithesis of God. Dark entities incarnate on planets like Earth simply to create evil, and they keep incarnating without ever going to the Other Side (as there is no negativity over there).

It's a shame that this world has to have darkness, but consider this: If there were no darkness, then we wouldn't need to incarnate. The whole idea of life is to spiritually learn and help light vanquish the dark. But don't confuse this planet with reality, as the real reality is the Other Side, where we exist for all eternity. Even if Earth falls, the people who are white entities—which, of course, includes mystical travelers—have won their own battle if they just convince one person that we have an all-loving Mother and Father.

Let me pause here to share a universal truth: *Everything in creation has a part of God within it, and that includes each one of us.* If our Creators were to destroy something in creation, They would be destroying a part of Themselves. While They may alter the form of something They created, They never get rid of the energy that They expended in creating it.

This explains a lot, for when we white entities physically die, our earthly form is instantly changed to our *real* form (which indeed does have a body), which exists on the Other Side for eternity. When dark entities die, however, they take a spirit form but never go to the Other Side. They're basically in a suspended state of waiting until they incarnate into another earthly life, which happens as quickly as possible. When the reincarnation schematic is finished, all dark entities and their creative energy will then be absorbed back into God, and all manifestation of evil and negativity will be ended.

Perhaps you're wondering, *Does this mean that God created evil?* The answer to that question is an emphatic *no*—all of creation was made with positive and loving energy. But when our Parents gave free will to Their creations, human beings brought negativity and evil to this world because of their flawed actions.

As our all-loving and all-knowing Mother and Father are perfect in every way, They naturally knew that this was going to happen. Thus, They allowed us plenty of opportunities to learn and help evolve our souls. It always comes down to the fact that we can't know what good is unless we've experienced evil, so we must learn about negativity in this school of learning called "Earth." To that end, the story of Lucifer and the other fallen angels is just an allegory to explain the human creations of evil and negativity.

To offer another example, we as parents always want our kids to succeed and be good at everything they do, but the personality of each individual child plays a great part in this scenario. We can guide, teach, and try to lead our sons and daughters by example; however, since we can't be with them 24 hours a day, the influences of others can divert them. Each soul is different, and his or her own free will determines what kind of person he or she will be.

Don't ever feel guilt about how your offspring turn out . . . you can only try to be a good parent and hope for the best. And keep in mind that dark entities incarnate in great numbers, so each and every one of you will be confronted with one or more of them in your lifetime. While they may not incarnate as one of your kids, I can almost guarantee that there is a dark entity somewhere in your family. Yet if you take the attitude of trying to learn from their actions, you'll find that the negative can become a positive.

My own mother was a dark soul, for instance, and I feel that I'm a better mother than she was because I didn't follow her advice and actions. So for those of you who have suffered abuse from a parent or other family member, learn from the experience and turn it into something that can work positively for you in your own life.

✝

Never mistake the fact that dark-souled entities are very seductive. They are insidious and seem to fit into your life like hands in gloves. They can come with great knowledge and, as my grandmother used to say, "With the ability to talk and beguile you with their silver tongues." If you get caught in their web, then the control and manipulation begins.

However, as a white-souled entity, you'll usually have a warning go off, as if something doesn't feel right. I don't mean the more commonplace sensation that you get when you're in a group or church and realize that it's not for you. This feeling is different . . . it's a loud alarm that begins to make you feel small and controlled. Even if someone just tells you that you can't ask questions, or that there are secrets you cannot know, it diminishes your worth.

Francine says that whatever you want to know can be answered—our Mother and Father don't play favorites or only let a few "chosen ones" know everything.

As I've said many times, dark entities are like heat-seeking missiles, and their entire focus is to diminish your estimation of self and annihilate the goodness within you. They want to uproot you, cause you to doubt yourself and lose faith, and make you depressed and ill. While they can commit every atrocity imaginable, their real aim is to shatter your soul and make you lose interest in life and spirituality.

I have a friend who was in a relationship with a dark entity, and she felt so smothered, as if he were an oxygen thief who made her feel that she couldn't breathe. In fact, what they do to you psychologically can result in all kinds of physical pain: You feel that you're "carrying" them (which manifests in back pain); they can make your "blood boil" (high blood pressure); you can't "stomach" them (ulcers); they "break your heart" (heart attack or similar concerns); you "don't want to hear" them (deafness); they "tire" you out (chronic fatigue); and on and on it goes.

Of course, there's plenty of disease in this world, but first look at your living conditions and really pay attention to how you feel when you're around your co-workers, friends, family members, mate, and even your own children. If negativity has indeed been implanted in your brain by a dark soul, there's an easy solution: Just take your index finger and press your forehead between your eyes and say, "Eject." You might be surprised by how much better you feel.

In more than 54 years of readings, I've seen so many people stay with dark entities because they feel it's their duty, their karma, or their spiritual evolvement. I completely understand this, as I came from a Catholic background and felt that you had to make the best of marriage, no matter what. My first husband was so physically and mentally abusive that I ended up in the hospital and almost died. I truly felt that I could make things right, but when it affected our children, then I knew I had to go.

When he came after our sons, I finally realized that I couldn't save him. It took a great deal of courage for me to escape this terrible situation, especially since my boys and I didn't have any money. Yet God always did provide for us, and anything was better than losing myself and getting so low that I didn't have the energy to escape at all.

This man later got drunk and ran over a boy on a bicycle and told so many lies (and still does). He went on to marry a woman who had to go into rehab for alcohol addiction, but he kept drinking—and then he apparently "got religion" and became a born-again Christian who judges everyone. It's very sad.

It may shock you to know that as advanced, spiritual, and protected as spirit guides or angels are, they don't want to be around dark souls. They don't put themselves in any negative environment unless they have to. So if that's the case, what makes us fragile humans think that we can convert or stave off all of their negativity? We can't . . . but we *can* learn and still survive the onslaught of darkness that we face in life by constantly fighting it and doing good.

Yes, we can protect ourselves, but why don't we just remove ourselves as much as possible from negativity altogether? After all, even if we're mystical travelers, we can't change or convert dark-souled entities. As Jesus said, "Don't cast your pearls before swine" (Matthew 7:6), so let's heed those profound words.

### How Mystical Travelers Can Help

Besides performing good acts, advanced souls are the only ones other than angels who can neutralize negativity and darkness. The Thrones and Principalities are God's army of angels, but because they haven't lived lives, mystical travelers have a greater understanding of the battle than they do. Advanced entities are the champions of saving planets from darkness, the crusaders and protectorates who help wherever and whenever they can.

They do have their own jagged mountains to climb; and almost all are scoffed at, ridiculed, or defamed in one way or another. But they're aware that life is short, no matter how long they live; that everything is transient and moving; and that nothing lasts forever. Since they've given up their will, they must be at the beck and call of God at any moment. Thanks to their mantles, they're ready to fight all injustices and darkness, but most of all, they're there to educate and impart knowledge.

Francine says, "Mystical travelers are in a direct category of their own, free to go to any place, time, or space. They are absolutely in an elevation of soul unto themselves." It seems that they're Mother and Father God's answer to dark entities and negativity. They don't fight them like angels do, but rather protect other people and give them courage when *they* must fight. Advanced souls have greater powers than dark entities do, but dark entities far outnumber them; thus, it really boils down to having enough mystical travelers to combat them.

Dark souls never wear out because this planet (the only real hell) is negative in nature, so it becomes a natural habitat for them. White entities do have a tendency to wear out faster because they're so outnumbered, and negativity is *not* their natural environment. Dark entities thrive on the negativity and just seem to go on and on; they're also very deceptive and can even pretend to be mystical travelers. However, true mystical travelers never cop out, bow out, or defect—they hang on against all adversity.

As you can see, Earth needs an incredible amount of these advanced souls. In order to defeat the horrendous problems of this world, it only makes sense that they're coming here in great numbers to battle darkness. Always remember that white-souled entities are stronger than dark-souled entities because the spirituality that they create and disseminate is truly a manifestation of the power of Mother and Father God . . . and no one is more powerful than They are.

I don't believe there was a battle between Satan and Saint Michael in the beginning, since Satan was only a symbol for dark entities that separated from God. Besides, just on a rational level, there are millions of archangels, and they all can't be named Michael. I feel that at the end of times, it will be the mystical travelers against the powers of darkness—advanced souls won't fight with swords or weapons, but will instead fill the world with so much truth and light that those who opt for the dark will have nowhere to hide. The old expression "The truth will set you free" is logically so true.

The dark side tries very hard to defeat mystical travelers, but they also have a certain amount of fear because advanced souls can call on Azna, the Mother God, and other protective and powerful resources. These can include minions of angels and other protectors, including loved ones who have passed over, or even members of the Council on the Other Side.

Dark entities fall into their own pits; the problem is that they always justify themselves because they're never wrong in their own eyes. Whereas we mission-life entities or mystical travelers often worry about being on track, or wish that we could have done certain things differently, this is stupid. Our charts are set, and we're either white or dark—we can never make a dark entity white or vice versa. Mystical travelers can't let anyone walk on their God center, but they must also encourage and be protective of other white entities who might not be as strong as they are. For example, I had to look out for my boys and protect them from their father. And although I never spoke ill of him (I didn't have to) and they carry his last name, my sons want nothing to do with that man.

Dark souls are robotic and have chosen to separate from God. As adamant as we white entities are to advance ourselves, they're just as adamant about trying to derail us and make us believe that advancement of the soul is false. They try to beguile us into thinking that we can do what we want without consequence, and they try to influence us (or let others do it) to go off track. Again, this has nothing to do with being part of a group, religion, or society— I've seen many mystical travelers who were Catholic, Jewish, Muslim, Buddhist, Protestant, and so on.

Raheim says, "The mystical traveler could be called a phenomenon that has occurred from the very conception of creation . . . but you will not get any black mark or retribution on your soul whether you accept being a mystical traveler or not.

"At the end of God's reincarnation schematic, even dark entities will find themselves being absorbed back into the uncreated mass of God, while the rest of us will keep our individual identities on the Other Side. They chose to separate, which was their ego and their freewill choice on the Other Side. God made everything perfect, but once we gained our free will, we decided to become white or dark souls. Dark-souled entities do serve a purpose: Besides creating negativity to learn from, they've also created a need for mystical travelers to dispel that negativity. Even with all their power, mystical travelers cannot turn dark entities white and shouldn't waste their time trying to do so. Don't even waste your Eight Keys on them—just bless them and let them go on their way."

Raheim also warns us to be careful of judging a dark entity because actions truly speak louder than words. Just because you don't like someone who's cranky or unkind doesn't necessarily mean that he or she is dark. There are lots of white entities who can be irritating because of what they've been through in life. There can be individuals you don't like, but don't let false pride or ego make you the judge and jury of a white entity who's just an irritant.

Dark entities have no feelings of guilt, and they're never wrong—*you are*. They hurt and don't care, and they never look back. They're full of malice and look down upon every race, creed, and sexual preference; many times they like to hide behind the Bible and just pick out the passages that suit them. Also be aware of those who seem to be holy and good and yet are illogical or spout falsehoods. These are the Jim Joneses, the David Koreshes, the Adolf Hitlers, the Saddam Husseins, and so forth. Their actions may seem to be reasonable and good at the time, but then they turn evil and gain control, beginning to manipulate and use others for their own purposes.

The good thing is that if there's anyone a dark entity can't bring down, it's a mystical traveler (or, really, any white entity). The mystical traveler has the tools of endurance to keep going onward, no matter what negative press, lies, or character assassinations are perpetrated upon them. Dark entities don't believe in God . . . they can't because they refuse to let light in. They put down prophets, celebrities, and even scientists who are trying to do good, yet they strangely have no problem asking for money to further their own causes.

### Conquering the Darkness

Even white entities can get caught up in the false propaganda that a dark entity can put forth—just look at Germany under Hitler or Iraq under Saddam—but they do usually come to their senses. Some who are misguided can slip from the light for a while, but they generally have it within their souls to right themselves. We've all experienced this in one way or another: Perhaps we were gullible enough to believe in someone or something we shouldn't have, but then our souls woke up and our lights shone brighter. Keep in mind that if we didn't know darkness for what it was, we couldn't combat it.

As Francine has said, "Every person should be taking their own control, rather than being taken control of." And when asked how we can neutralize negative energy, she replied, "By knowledge . . . and that is to be aware of the enemy, which is the dark side. The good news is that the veil is thinning between my side and the Earth plane, and spirit guides and angels can help more." At my lectures and during my appearances on *Montel*, I've been noticing that more people are seeing their guides, passed-over loved ones, and angels.

On the other hand, the dark side also sees the thinning of the veil and is attacking with vigor. So mystical travelers *can* fail, but they almost never intend to do so, and intent and motive are everything. There are accidents, words said in haste, not making it to a deathbed, even letting loose with a temper tantrum in a moment of stress . . . so often I see people taking on failure and guilt for something they have no control over.

We tend to forget that others wrote their own charts; we also can't take responsibility for dark-souled entities who are friends or family members, for they may be there to test our tolerance or patience. It's important to acknowledge that sometimes we simply have to go on our way and let them deal with their own charts.

Dark entities can make you feel futile, depressed, and even sick—this is what we refer to as a psychic attack. They can also send negative energy from afar, so it's not just the ones around you who are guilty. Great greed, great injustice, poor judgment, and even extensive communication (propaganda) used in the wrong way can exacerbate darkness.

My advice is to ignore them, for the truth will come out eventually. No one is correct in all things (except, of course, for God), so don't let such individuals deflect you from doing good. Keep your aura clean by surrounding yourself with the white light of the Holy Spirit or by visualizing mirrors or a silver netting all around you. Use positive defensive visualizations to defeat negative attacks, and always ask for God's protection. Also protect your home and loved ones and even the world by putting white light and silver netting around it all.

✟

If mystical travelers get in a position of feeling shrouded by darkness, they can reaffirm the Eight Golden Keys; in doing so, their auras can go out 30, 40, or even 50 feet (and more if they concentrate) to dissolve the darkness. Their ability to dissipate and dissolve darkness is one of their primary weapons in assisting humanity.

Unlike other people, mystical travelers have to profess their beliefs and can only help their fellow men and women do good. This doesn't necessarily mean that they have to preach, because they can also profess by their actions, but they do have to respond to others if asked. Advanced souls must go outward in deed and word to have their blessed effect—what would be the use to have them go inward, for then they couldn't spread good and light? As Christ said so beautifully, "Let your light so shine before men, that they may see your good works, and glorify your Father which is in heaven" (Matthew 5:16).

The Council and guides take a somewhat dim view of entities living in total solitude. Of course if we go through grief, hardship, or pain, we may very well pull in and live in a desert period for a while; however, to go through an entire lifetime as a hermit is a waste because our lights should radiate outward. We can rejuvenate for a certain period, but then we have to get up and start on our mystical-traveler journey again. How long can we keep hidden something beautiful that gives joy to others? Isn't the first thing we want to do is share our knowledge and spirituality?

The following quotes are from Francine:

- "Hate is not something that needs to be shared as much as love is, for God and creation are love."

- "When you are in love, you want to share it with everyone."

- "When you are in a state of hate or vengeance, you are morose, internal, and sick."

How often do you hear someone say that they're in a state of hate? If mystical travelers feel negative, this can be natural because they're human, but if the feeling persists it may well be a sign that darkness has dimmed them. If this happens, they must elevate themselves and polish themselves up, so to speak, by using the Eight Keys and strengthening and reaffirming their paths as mystical travelers.

Everyone can feel when you're down or dim, just as they can tell when you're bright and alert. They don't have to see it; it's an intuitive knowledge that something isn't right when you're down. But when you reaffirm your light, it gets brighter, and your aura explodes into brilliant colors.

✢ ✢ ✢

# CHAPTER NINE

# THE SEVEN RAYS OF GOD

It's amazing how many times the numbers six and seven come into play in creation: There are seven levels on the Other Side, which is itself often called "the sixth dimension," and there are the six levels of soul advancement. Then there are seven days in which the world was supposedly created, although it was actually done in an instant. We have to quit giving our Creators a timeline, as everything with Them always was and will always be.

We run into the number seven again when mystical travelers become privy to "the Seven Rays of God." These Rays are not to be confused with anything else that's given to mystical travelers, as they're separate and unique unto themselves. They each pertain to creation and how we came into being, what we looked like, our themes, our created purpose, and so forth—the Rays seem to be woven throughout all of theology, even from the so-called beginning of what we call "time."

Since Mother and Father God are equal-opportunity employers, anyone can have access to the Seven Rays, but mystical travelers specifically take them on to align with creation and the force of the Godhead. Advanced souls receive them more deeply, with the firm knowledge that they have to take these tools out into the world.

Although you've come this far with me, I understand if you still have reservations about being a mystical traveler. This is perfectly all right. Even if becoming an advanced entity isn't for you, the spiritual information you're getting in this book will enhance your life. If you're brave, you'll want to advance your own soul as much as you can; if you're not, it won't diminish you one bit in the eyes of our Parents.

It's especially important that you use these Seven Rays, which could also be known as "the Seven Holy Vibrations," in meditation so that you can more easily complete your journey on the Earth plane. When you keep surrounding yourself with them, they become deeper and more resonant for everyone around you. Also, the more you're aware of them, the more aware darkness is . . . and stays away. In other words, dark entities don't have access to the Seven Rays, which gives you quite an edge to combat such souls. Again, it just goes to show that light is always supreme over dark.

Now more than ever, the world is in such chaos that it's moving full-speed ahead toward the end of this schematic. By asking to go into these seven vibratory stages, you can advance and purify your soul and become a beam of light in a dark, negative world. They may not be for everyone, but for those of you who are spiritually advanced, they can be a boon to your soul.

The more spiritual you become, the farther the Rays spread out, and the more knowledge you seem to infuse—and, of course, knowledge will set you free. I don't mean false knowledge here, but rather what your soul responds to, or to use a more common expression, your "gut feeling."

It's so gratifying to me when I hear people say, "I always knew in my heart that what you were saying was right, Sylvia, but I either couldn't put it into words or I was worried about what others would feel about me . . . I didn't want to stand out as being crazy or an oddball." There has to be a reason why so many of us end up coming to the truth—I think it's because in the process, we're able to receive the vital information our Mother, our angels and spirit guides, and our passed-over loved ones are sending us.

When it comes to using the Rays, there are two quotes from Francine that are definitely appropriate. The first one is: "In your written record from God, what you are to perfect in this life is to follow your individual program and themes to advance for Them." The second is: "When you have the knowledge that you can vibrate positively, you are evolving, and that is the meaning of your own schematic." While these words may seem simplistic, they're so true.

You see, using the Seven Rays of God won't change your themes or life's plan—but it will enhance them and make them stronger. You will also have abilities that you didn't have before, such as healing, bringing about harmony, and cutting through negativity. It's really easy to use the Rays, colors, and vibrations; but humans make things so complicated sometimes. Know that simply using the information in this chapter is enough . . . it *will* make things happen.

### The Seven Rays Explained

I'm often asked, "Why are people so cruel, jealous, politically undermining, and just plain discourteous?" I'll agree that lots of folks just don't seem to care these days. The news; the daily stress; the financial crunches; and the breakdown of family, neighbors, and people who used to stick together have sent them running like lemmings to the sea. And it's getting even more frantic, leading to an increase in depression, fatigue, and feelings of futility. Of course those who take steps to protect themselves aren't affected by the "negativity buildup" that others suffer.

If you embrace even a small amount of the protective measures in this book, they will not only make your soul advance, but they'll make your life happier, too. The Rays should always be used—not just when you think you might be going into battle against darkness, but in everyday life as well. It certainly can't hurt to protect yourself from negativity 24/7.

The colors of the Seven Rays of God also correspond to the "chakras" (or energy vortexes) of the body, and they can emanate from those places. What follows is a detailed and thorough examination of each of them:

**1. The first Ray is the energy of creative force.** Also known as the "Thought Ray," this is the highest vibration, as it is a direct emanation from our Creators. For our finite minds' understanding, this is the "beginning" of Their thought force, which created all of creation.

It's hard for us to think that everything always was, but our human brains do comprehend "beginning," "middle," and "end." While this so-called thought of Mother and Father God became flesh, it still proves that we've always existed, be it in Their mind or outside as individual beings. To use a simplistic analogy, it's almost like pregnancy: We know that the baby exists in the mother, but it hasn't really come into full being yet. (As an aside, if a baby isn't born alive—or at all—then the soul doesn't enter.)

God's thought comes in the vibration of silver light, which goes along with the silver columns that we can carry from the tops of our heads to the tips of our toes. We can plant these columns everywhere, which mystical travelers are especially great at doing. In fact, there's a prayer that goes along with the receiving of the Rays that helps to keep your ego in check:

*"I ask that my 'I am' be lined up with the Rays. I ask that my 'I am' be lined up with Mother God and that the silver light comes all the way through all negativity to me. I ask that I stay on my intended track for my chart and that it never deviates."*

Now, when we use the first Ray, we're privy to seeing the Godhead, which we should know or understand because we can always sense God if we pay attention. However, we can't see or feel our Father for long because taking shape is not His natural state of being, and He is so powerful that He only chooses to hold a form for a short period of time. As Francine says, "God the Father can take a form but does so only briefly, whereas Azna the Mother chooses to constantly hold one." This isn't because She is lower in power—She just becomes more humanized, while His vibration is more ethereal.

This Ray is really the emanation of our Parents, just in different form and attributes. The "thought" in the first vibration splits, which comes from the Male and the Female and Creation and Form, and that then goes on into infinity.

The first Ray is all of life and creation, and you can surround yourself with, and bathe in, its glow. (Make sure to visualize these Rays and colors as coming through the top of the head and through every organ, as it will keep stress at bay.)

**2. The second Ray is when the actual thought becomes flesh.** You see, after its creation, the thought is now put into separate species, each having its own identity, just as all living things have their own unique differences.

The only entities who don't incarnate are angels and members of the Council on the Other Side, who help us with our charts. The Council consists of very advanced entities who help us make decisions—and while they give us all kinds of advice, they never judge. We might not always hear what we want to from them, but they do always counsel us on what would be the best path for us to take.

This reminds me of when my first great love came into my life. I was in college and with him for just a few short months, until I found out that he was married (albeit separated). Although I still wanted to be with him, Francine told me that the Council said it wasn't right for him. So, with every ounce of strength I could muster up inside of me, I sent this man back to his wife. It was the right thing to do, but not a day has gone by in all these years when he doesn't pop into my mind. But then I tell myself that there's always our Home, where we can meet those loved ones who just weren't for this life, no matter how much our emotions wanted it.

The color of the second Ray is a very dark blue. Francine says, "It's very hard to describe these colors because they're alive—they actually breathe and vibrate from your life force and from God. Within these Rays, as they come from God, they are darkest in the center or the part that is closest to your body, or your 'matter,' as we call it. Then it emanates in a spiral around you and lightens in color toward the end."

As a mystical traveler, you can use these Rays to dispel darkness or negativity in other people, whether they know it or not. If you see two people fighting verbally or physically, for instance, you can mentally put a blue light through them to bring them peace. You're not doing them any harm because you're only protecting them—you're not trying to convert them or change their beliefs in any way. (It's also good to use this technique when driving because there is so much road rage out there.)

Even if you're not a mystical traveler, you can use the Rays if you want to combat illness, negativity, and the like; it's just that advanced souls have more control over them and can direct them better. Keep in mind that God doesn't play favorites, and all is available to everyone. Much like anyone can play the piano, not every person will be a concert pianist . . . the same can be said about mystical travelers.

Visualizing the blue light around you brings about peace and tranquility.

**3. The third Ray is used to really disperse negative energy.** Like the first and second Rays, the third one illustrates that thoughts are things; so before we go any further, we must realize that since we're part of the Divine, we have great power.

Even though we've written our charts, we can minimize traumas or even get through them more quickly by using our thoughts. (We also have the power to create miracles.) In addition, we can escalate our finances by affirming abundance, which doesn't mean "just getting by." Unfortunately, we often become so frantic that we keep away the one thing we desire the most. It's the same as when negativity is so thick that nothing good can come through—our desert period lasts longer or makes such a barrier that what we need or want can't get to us. Yet as Francine explains, "If we remove an obsessive need, then abundance or our wish can come through."

The third Key is emerald green in color, which is the hue of the healer. And while everyone can heal, mystical travelers have a special inside track: They can call on the Council; the angels, especially the phyla of Archangels, Powers, Thrones, and Municipalities; and even the Sword of Azna that, with Her help, can replace illness with health. In fact, Azna's sword is able to cut through any kind of negativity—not so much for those using it, but for others. This is a good thing, for it's often very difficult for advanced entities to not only live their own charts, but to help others with theirs as well.

I don't want you to feel that mystical travelers are in any way members of an elitist club—no one meets, and the oath is only between those advanced souls and God. If you don't choose to be such a soul, you can be just as evolved in Mother and Father God's eyes, and They don't love certain individuals more than others. And if you do become a mystical traveler, never get the idea that you're better than anyone or are one of God's so-called chosen, for it's *your* need to ascend, not Theirs, that calls you to take on the mantle.

The color green is a symbol of reproduction, life, and growth; as well as being the hue of healing and getting rid of negativity.

**4. The fourth Ray helps you renew your commitment to give your will to God,** in order to get to your personal level of perfection. Always with the help of the Council, you map out what you're going to do and what it will take to get there. Even mystical travelers have to travel the roads of life, some of which are washed out or bumpy—every single one of us needs all the help we can get to get us through these rocky roads of life.

Mystical travelers have all the Rays' colors emanating from their auras, and along with Azna's sword, they're very effective opponents against any and all negativity. This Ray uses the color orange, which is my favorite because it doesn't have the anger of red. It's not that red is somehow bad, but orange is softer and represents dusk and dawn to me . . . the beginning and the end.

Also, think about how many religious groups use orange—such as Buddhists and Tibetan monks. Like the setting sun, the orange robes of these monks signify life giving and renewal. This doesn't mean that you'll be able to bring the dead back to life by using this color, but orange's vibratory aura *can* dispel depression. In most cases, it will even help people who have given up hope and are in the grips of feeling that they want to end their lives.

The fourth Ray is like your personal symphony. Some of you may have heard me speak of the music of the spheres (which permeates the Other Side) . . . well, this is what I've been describing. Creation is not just flesh, trees, animals, mountains, rivers, and the like; it's a living, breathing force that permeates everything that's alive. The music of the spheres and the colors of the Rays are just prime examples of that energy.

As you use these living and colorful Rays, you can accomplish things that you never knew were possible. You don't need the ego satisfaction of always seeing what you've done, but you'll know that you've done the right and holy thing. When you *do* hear about the good you've done, remember that it came from God—always keep your vow to Them in the foreground of your mind, remembering that you're only a vessel or tube for Their energy to go through.

**5. The fifth Ray has to do with knowledge**—not only how much information you've acquired in each lifetime, but also how much you can avidly search for as a mystical traveler. Knowledge is all around; if you negate it, that's one of the ways you can miss your goal of making your spirit grow, regardless of whatever religion or creed you subscribe to.

No matter what path you take to increase your evolvement and spirituality, you must always be in the state of acquiring knowledge. But what you find won't all be truthful or useful—you have to separate the wheat from the chaff and keep what works for *you*.

After all, beliefs are not necessarily truths, and there are many who believe erroneously because they've been taught erroneously. The more knowledge you obtain, the more you'll be able to discern falsehood from truth. Truth will feel good and make your soul soar!

What's magnificent is that the more you learn, the more knowledge you'll hunger for, even on the Other Side. When everybody begins to ascend higher, then all the information they've gathered will strangely begin to converge to be an ultimate truth, and spirituality will become the umbrella over all religions.

Mystical travelers always migrate toward the ultimate truth. Such truth is universal, very simplistic, and full of understanding —and forever devoid of jealousy, greed, vengeance, and malice. You can find the ultimate truth despite all the odds . . . you just have to keep your "eyes on the prize," as it were. This means never hurting anyone with malice aforethought; and while you must always strive to do good works and deeds, you also have to remember that you're human.

The one thing you can fight the most in your evolvement to be a mystical traveler is yourself. You don't have to be perfect or some sort of holy person—it's much more important to think of yourself as a puzzle piece that links everything together. If your piece breaks, you diminish the other pieces. This not only gives you spiritual importance, but it also keeps you connected and away from total isolation.

Garner knowledge from *everywhere*—be it from people, books, belief systems, schools, or just current everyday events—because it's all part of this world. Yet make sure the knowledge fits you, or else you'll begin to live under someone else's shelter and won't perform in your own way. You must have the freedom to express yourself, be the true you, and develop and evolve in your own way . . . and this is where religion has tragically gone off track.

By not letting all people follow their paths in their own way, religion has tried to fit everyone into one train of thought or type of dogma according to its beliefs, functioning like an iron maiden that pierces the individuality of the soul's advancement. If people tried to escape or challenge it, they were branded as "sinful" or "bad."

You can be the thought, you are made flesh, and you can evolve. *Evolution* means nothing more than the state of becoming flesh to learn for God. If you choose to become an entity who wishes to level up and become a mystical traveler, you can stay on track simply by gathering knowledge and staying within God's Rays. In the process, you automatically form the Rays within your aura, and that's what many people feel or sense.

The fifth Ray's color is mauve, and surrounding yourself with it will help with your pursuit of knowledge.

**6. The sixth Ray is known for activation, experience, and protection.** By utilizing this Ray, you're putting into use your experience—you're more or less activating what you've come to know so far in your evolvement. If you're on your last life, you'll feel bits and pieces of every emotion, be it big or small, as well as different events that you might not have gone through or finished experiencing fully in your past incarnations.

This is the protection Ray, which is white in color, and we can use it to take care of others. Even if we have to experience many things in life, it helps make them easier to go through when we have the white light around us, which is why we always need to surround ourselves with the white light of the Holy Spirit.

All the Rays neutralize negative energy, but this one *really* dissipates it. As these Rays build on each other, they begin to work individually and collectively—so the more you use them, the stronger they become.

Some may think that the first Ray (the thought of God) is the most important, but actually, the thought is very embryonic. The sixth Ray is vital because out of this life form, you've made of yourself who and what you'd like to be, in order to experience for God. Some of you will choose to be a mystical traveler or mission-life entity, or just a white soul who gets to the Other Side and gives glory to God . . . it really doesn't matter because it's all for Them.

**7. The seventh Ray is the culmination of everything you've ever done in all your lives,** as well as what you've experienced on the Other Side. It's the last hurrah, so to speak, in which you go back and get the full mantle of mystical traveler. Does that mean the first one you took wasn't permanent? No, of course not. This second mantle is simply richer and more permanent, as it's sealed by Mother God.

So after this incarnation is over, you'll rest and take over your duties on the Other Side. And then after that, you'll be called upon to go to other planets. If it seems that you'll never stop . . . well, that's why you're known as a mystical *traveler*. You'll continually carry with you the mantle of salvation so that you can help, heal, and even pass on some of the Rays to others.

The seventh Ray's color is not set in stone as the others are, so it can be any color you want it to be. Most mystical travelers pick gold or purple because these colors are generally associated with royalty and advanced spirituality, but choose whatever you feel best fits your aura. As I've mentioned, I really like the color orange, but I also use purple and gold because they all suit me.

✧

Mystical travelers won't go off track, but they can just stop and become immobile—and the only time there's a danger of failure is the time between the fourth and fifth Rays. The other Rays are put in place by God, but when you get to the fifth Ray, you're on your own. It's up to your own initiative to seek out information; if you don't, you become stagnant or disenchanted, or you can be led astray by someone else. This could also be called the Ray that tests you, for if you stop teaching and searching for information, you're in a state of shutting down.

If you quit learning and seeking or caring about experiencing, your body and mind have no new information coming in— when this happens, your body becomes weakened and your mind becomes depressed. Senility sets in because you've become so inert that your mind thinks you're dead. Remember, whether you're a mystical traveler or not, "If you don't use it, you lose it."

Of course you'll get tired and can be tested, but don't be lured into a state of believing that you know enough or that your knowledge is so great that you don't need to go any further. You might find yourself in a state of mind where you don't need things to be any harder, or you want to stay right where you are. Well, you have to push yourself beyond this point. You'll still be a mystical traveler if you don't, but you will not have fulfilled your true completeness of purpose.

Even the whitest of entities will stumble and fall, but true avatars will pick themselves up and go on. Keep in mind that the oath you took wasn't just to God—it was to yourself, too. So if you do give up, there will be no other way to advance your soul but to live another life to fulfill your mystical-traveler training.

This is a far more serious oath than any other, carrying so much weight that we might even say that it's written on "God's scroll." Even most entities who've committed suicide (unless this was done out of malice or spite) don't have to come back unless they choose to, but if mystical travelers fail to keep searching and growing, they definitely have to come back. It's very important to be aware of these pitfalls so that you can overcome them.

### Strengthening the Rays

Someone once asked me how we can strengthen our Keys and Rays. Well, Francine said that using them in tandem with our chakras can be very helpful: "If you start at the crown chakra and work your way down the main meridian of the body, you can cleanse your chakras with meditation. It doesn't take long and will do two things: It balances your physical body with your spirit; and it helps you stay on track and fulfill your duties."

You'll also find it effective to go over the Eight Keys once a week and see where you can better your fortitude, mercy, honesty or honor, loyalty, gratitude, psychic or healing ability, levity, and great or grand intelligence (infused knowledge). Then you should thread the Seven Rays through your body, remembering as you do what they stand for, and asking if there's more you can do to enhance others' lives. You can also plant light columns around people, as well as surround them with the Rays.

While you ought to use all of the Rays, it's great to pick one that feels right to you, that resonates in your soul, or that is your own signature color. I personally prefer the silver Ray—even though my favorite color is orange, I use silver more to protect people or help them pass over. I also use green if I don't feel well or if someone else is ill. I've had people tell me at lectures or even in the audience at *Montel* that they see silver all around me—as for Montel himself, his aura really radiates gold. (Dark entities will either emit a dark muddy color or none at all, and their eyes are hard like marble or those of Charles Manson.)

The Rays can emanate from everyone, but not with the power that the mystical travelers do. These advanced entities walk around banded with all the colors close to their bodies; however, if darkness or negativity comes in, then the Rays begin to shoot out of them.

When you get up in the morning, your colored Rays may be too close to your body. Many times this is a subconscious need for protection, which indicates that you're too stressed or depleted. While the Rays stay strong when they're close, they become even stronger when they emanate from your body. So when you go to bed at night, ask that your Rays spread out in front of you in the morning and you'll feel much better. The Rays will always give you energy, but they'll give you even more when you spread them out.

If you find yourself in an environment where there's a lot of stress or negativity, you can emanate your Rays throughout the whole room. Whenever I do a lecture, hold a salon, or appear on Montel's show, I ask that my Rays encompass the entire area, along with anyone who's watching on TV. I ask my angels to take any Ray that will help them, be it peace, knowledge, health, or what have you.

You can increase the power of your Rays by pushing them out and then bringing them in. It's like a muscle: The more you exercise it, the more you increase its strength and flexibility. As you do this with your Rays, they'll get brighter. It shows the age-old truth that what you give out really does come back to you, just like love.

†

Now, let's say you come across an individual who's either mentally or physically ill. That's a perfect opportunity to call on your emerald green Ray and say, "Increase my green Ray, but let all of them blend into this person." You can also let the Rays blend into your children, no matter how old they are. If they're getting into trouble, use orange, for it can be used to complete things that are negative or need to be finished.

The Rays can also work wonders on autism and Alzheimer's disease because both trap people in their minds. Yet the souls who come in this way are very advanced; you'll never see weak souls come into bodies that have to fight through some type of handicap. They're very spiritual and help us all advance.

God has given me the ability to searchlight these wonderful minds, and I can usually sense and even see what they're thinking. It's almost as if I can get in the locked door to their minds, and they can follow me out the way I came in. It's certainly one door that I can open . . . and if I do it to one, what's to say that they all won't swing open? Especially when used by the mystical traveler, the Rays can indeed be the keys that open many a locked door.

To utilize and strengthen your Rays, try to make the following conditioned response every day: "God, help me with my Rays by flowing through them. Also, please carry negativity away on them, especially those that come from the Mother God."

A shorter version is to simply say every morning, "God, let the Rays flow through me." By praying and asking or making affirmations, it does make the Seven Rays of God stronger—but what amazes me is we forget that our Parents know our wants and needs even before we do. Yet prayer takes us closer to Them, and since thoughts are things, we can absolutely evoke our Mother to intervene and help us when the going gets too tough.

### The Guardianship of the Mind

As you know, the search for knowledge never ends, not even on the Other Side, so the Seven Rays of God will remain fortified as long as you follow the Eight Keys and keep seeking. And the more spiritual you become, the more you'll get into what's called "the guardianship of the mind."

Like its name suggests, the guardianship can be like a barrier that keeps others out. When you've come this far spiritually, the gates open, and you're able to access the Other Side's Akashic Records, where all knowledge exists. Here is where you can find information on your past lives, as well as data on history, theology, and acts that humankind has done or been involved with. Each link leads to another, which opens up other doors to more knowledge . . . thus, you can't help but elevate your psychic ability. The guardianship also enables you to assist other people like you never have before, and it allows you to easily discern truth from falsehood.

The Seven Rays of God are related to Carl Jung's concept of the "collective unconsciousness," for he claimed that it is in this place where everything is linked and can be tuned into. No matter what you call it, though, we *are* all linked. The securers of knowledge who are mystical travelers know how to tap into the total unconscious, or in this case, the consciousness of all humankind. This allows them to know the reason for their charts and their behavior—that is, why they've had joys and heartaches—and they understand the whole picture.

The best way to teach the methods of what you've learned is to communicate them through word and example. You can even use exercises, although if you do, you ought to make up your own—and even encourage others to do the same—as it's more personal that way. But this all should only be used with the idea that you're now reaching upward for the guardianship of the mind to open; once it does, it can help you with illness and past-life phobias.

Each action does link up to make every life understandable, illustrating how and why people are the way they are. The guardianship also gives us a full comprehension of why there seems to be so much inequity in the world, and we're also shown various charts. This, of course, gives us the knowledge of why life seems unfair and things are the way they are.

Rather than thinking that we have unjust and unfair Creators, we can see for ourselves why people make the choices they do—it has nothing to do with Them being vengeful or picking and choosing who will suffer for no reason. Even in this day of enlightened spirituality, people still blame God for the death of a loved one or any misfortune we suffer. To point to Them, when we're the ones who chose our charts to advance our souls, is wrong. We simply can't learn if we're only exposed to happiness.

I'm reminded of the conversation I had recently with a woman who said that she thought this life would be perfect, and she was very upset that it wasn't.

I responded, "Then you shouldn't have come here. This is a very negative place, but you're here to learn."

Does this mean that everything is terrible in life? Of course not. Nevertheless, we're all going to go through sorrow as well as joy, for most of the time we learn much more from the adversities of life.

✝ ✝ ✝

# CHAPTER TEN

# ANSWERS
# AND INSIGHT
# FROM FRANCINE

My spirit guide Francine has conducted at least 30 trances on the subject of mystical travelers, possibly spending more time on it than she has on cell memory, dreams, or angels. The reason for this is because some of my ministers went over my trilogy of *The Journey of the Soul* with a fine-tooth comb and began to ask about it in great detail. As I've gleaned from the transcripts of these trances, she seemed to be a little reluctant to give out the information at first, and of course that only made everyone want it more.

The research trances were held in Seattle and San Jose, and my guide informed everyone at that time that there wouldn't be too many people (outside of the ministers, that is) who'd want to know about mystical travelers for many years. As it turned out, she was right: It has been over a decade since she presented this information, which the world wasn't ready for yet. However, I feel the time is right to share much of it with you now.

The following are questions Francine was asked while in trance, along with her answers:

**Q: Is life easier for a mystical traveler?**

A: No, but the highs *are* more wondrous. However, the lows of life can also be extremely difficult. What happens is that through these peaks and valleys, you'll always find that mystical travelers come to a meadow—that is, they gain a great deal of peace of mind in this life. All the insignificant phobias and needless worries they deal with (such as loneliness, poverty, and illness) seem to diminish and drop away, because by giving their will to our Mother and Father, they know with all certainty that They are with them. So when it comes to any problem, they'll always survive and come out winners.

**Q: How many mystical travelers are there?**

A: There are now two million and counting, with more coming in each day. There are also millions on other planets throughout the universe.

**Q: What were mystical travelers before they became such advanced entities?**

A: A few mystical travelers have always been this way, as they were created as such by our Parents. The majority, however, came from all walks of life and many different occupations, but they had one thing in common: They all wanted more spirituality. Most mystical travelers are Gnostic in nature because they're seekers of wisdom and truth, regardless of what religion they practice on Earth. They can be homebodies who do good works; or they may be philosophers, teachers, businesspeople, artisans, lecturers, leaders, writers, and so forth. In other words, they can be anybody and anything.

Each individual entity can choose to take the mantle or negate it without judgment, and only our Creators know who will choose to be a mystical traveler. No individual who refrains from searching for more would have the need, want, or longing to became an advanced soul . . . and please remember that there are very, very good and saintly people who don't choose to take on the mantle.

**Q: Is the mystical traveler genetically presupposed?**

A: No, it is a chosen path in any lifetime . . . whether he or she knows the proper name of "mystical traveler" or not, anyone can always be one. Also, it's not only mystical travelers who opt for more difficult incarnations to help them fulfill their missions —many other white souls choose challenging life charts to quickly elevate their advancement in spirituality. So I'm sure that if it's not in their conscious mind, somewhere in all white entities' superconsciousness lies the ability to take on the mantle if they so desire.

The mystical traveler may pick a family of teachers or authors or any situation that would give him or her an outlet to be better prepared for a life as such an advanced soul. For example, Sylvia chose to incarnate into a family of writers, teachers, and psychics so as to give her an environment that would help her fulfill her duties. She also picked an "option example" life, as most mystical travelers do, which is usually their last existence on a particular planet. This makes sense, as many souls save the worst for last because of the added experience they've already garnered.

No one should ever feel or think that they'd be turned away from becoming a mystical traveler—*no one* is unworthy. It's so simple to become a mystical traveler . . . you just have to ask.

[**Sylvia:** Later on in the book, I'll give you an affirmation prayer that Francine shared with me, which really seals the mystical-traveler contract.]

**Q: By asking, do we gain more spirituality?**

A: Yes, because you're then advanced enough to know that you're searching for the next spiritual step. But keep in mind that you must also be dedicated and willing to work for spirituality by learning and doing. You have to put out some effort—and especially have a real desire with pure motive—to want to become more spiritual. Think about this: Would you rather drink plain or more purified water? Both will quench your thirst, but the pure water is more satisfying and makes you feel better.

**Q: Are some people elected to be mystical travelers?**

A: Not really. God certainly made some of them in what we might call the "beginning" of creation, and these entities are special creations. Having said that, everyone has the power and capability to advance in spirituality and become mystical travelers. Some people will never choose to do so, which is perfectly fine—not everyone wants to be a CEO. And with all the good that comes with being a mystical traveler, it's no walk in the park. The life can be hard because God's will takes precedence over all, and living in a human environment where capitalism and temptation reign supreme can greatly test the individual's fortitude and commitment.

**Q: Can I learn enough to become a mystical traveler?**

A: It has very little to do with what facts you've collected. When you become a mystical traveler, the main by-product will be *infused* knowledge from God, which is enough for you to complete your mission. It has more to do with the glorious sanction of the soul, as sometimes a learned person can overanalyze and forget that the simple truths are often blatantly clear and not hidden away somewhere.

Consider the fact that Jesus was a carpenter by trade, yet he brought a message of love and forgiveness to the world, saying that it was so simple that a child could understand it. The very act of giving up your will becomes a source of God's Divine act of imbued knowledge. As you embark upon an eternity of glorious adventure and discovery, you'll learn so much in the process.

**Q: Can one make a false declaration to be a mystical traveler?**

A: No, for it's a true commitment. But for the sake of argument, let's say that someone comes in and tries to take on the mantle because of a whim. Even if they say it but don't mean it in their heart and soul, the mantle won't drop. This is usually the person who's hopped everywhere looking for a fast fix, much like taking a diet pill yet still eating everything in sight. It's like saying that you're a Christian, but not living by the teachings of Christ.

You must remember that our Creators know everything: our deeds, our hearts, and our intentions. Mystical travelers' oaths are written on their souls—not by words, but by their own souls' dedication to evolve higher for Them. It's a blessing bestowed by God to let the mantle drop.

**Q: Can the mystical traveler be judged as a false prophet?**

A: Being a mystical traveler has very little to do with prophecy. The only prophet you have is yourself: Your belief and your covenant with Mother and Father God are all that matters. Certainly you may find other mystical travelers who are on a high level of knowledge, with advanced psychic ability, but remember that our Parents only help to open spiritual doors. In other words, the "ultimate door opener" in your sphere is you.

**Q: Can the mystical-traveler calling be ignored?**

A: Yes, but those who do so will be bothered terribly, feeling that they've missed the so-called spiritual boat. Usually, though, at some time in their lives they're going to heed that call, whether they know the name for it or not. After all, many people are mystical travelers but don't know the proper label. It really doesn't matter—although it's better to use the correct terminology because it gives the soul solace to find what's been missing. It's like when you're sick and know what you have and how to treat it: You feel more at peace than if you didn't know what was going on.

**Q: Can the mantle be dropped at any time?**

A: It could, but that's a moot point because you wouldn't want to. Also, you've hopefully prayed and concentrated on becoming a mystical traveler long enough to know that it's your destiny. After all, you wouldn't be seeking higher spirituality if it wasn't in your chart to have the option to take it on.

In the will of the mystical traveler lies the synergy to work toward a specific end, which is to simply make a *positive* difference in the world. He or she truly lives by the motto "What does not destroy me, makes me stronger." But to be specific, if a person drops the mantle, he or she never had it in the first place.

**Q: Can the mantle be given away to anyone else?**

A: No, as it is personally yours and no one else's. Please take responsibility here: Don't listen to anything or anyone but your own soul. If what I'm saying doesn't feel right to you, for instance, then it isn't. You can be given all the Keys and Rays, but it's you who must accept the mantle or turn the corner—no one else can do it for you. Also, if and when you do make the commitment, it becomes the essence of you.

**Q: Can advanced entities go off track or follow the wrong path?**

A: They don't go off track, but they might go on the shoulder of the road once in a while. Yet mystical travelers seem to reenergize faster and will step back on that road faster than most. They always want to stay on course to do God's will.

If they're caught in some type of strange society or group, then they may be fooled for a time. But with God's protection and their ever-opening senses, they'll back up and readjust. They won't buy into the falsehoods some groups put out, such as that demons will possess them or that they have to give away all of their money to be saved. So, although mystical travelers can deviate for a time, they eventually realize that this certain group or occult organization is insanity, and they leave in order to follow the right road again.

**Q: Can mystical travelers ever be deceived?**

A: Yes, because they still have to learn. Taking on the mantle doesn't take away the life charts that they constructed to learn from; it's actually more of an overlay on the charts.

It seems to be somewhat paradoxical to say that advanced souls have to put up more barriers against dark entities but also let down barriers to help everyone they can. When they let down those barriers, many times they become fooled, and darkness comes in with all its seductiveness. The good news is that mystical travelers are quicker to discern dark energy and even have more power to get out of a situation and make it right. They're definitely infused with a greater ability to be psychic, to be aware, to heal, and to create peace.

**Q: Are mystical travelers more prone to psychic attacks and picking up negativity from others?**

A: Well, they certainly are attacked more by skeptics. No one minds open-minded skeptics, but those who are atheistic or agnostic, as well as mean-spirited, will attack with venom because they want to rule a godless world. However, while mystical travelers can take hits of negativity and psychic attack, it's not more than what anyone else faces. As you know, there's a hierarchy of dark entities that wants to bring God and spirituality down; and as the world gets whiter, they get darker. They can be in high places or even in your family, but you must be brave and persevere. Mystical travelers just keep going against all adversity—they suffer the slings and arrows and lies because they know that in the end, all will find their way to God, and dark souls will be absorbed back into our ever-loving God.

**Q: Do mystical travelers have doubts?**

A: Of course, for it's human to have doubts. I believe that with any commitment, especially one as binding as this one is, it would be egocentric *not* to have some concern. Even when you start a new job or go to a strange country, you have doubts, so why would something as important as this task not make you feel the same way? But the learning and sense of spirituality that begins immediately will take away those doubts very quickly.

You will never find mystical travelers who feel that they have totally arrived. All advanced souls are constantly in the state of becoming more evolved, but they can never learn *everything*, since they're not God. Yet they can continually work to bring God's love to all of humanity.

## Q: Do mystical travelers drift away?

A: No. Any mystical travelers who think that they've dropped the mantle or have denied it will always come back to their rightful path. There will be such an unbelievable yearning in their souls—worse than any feelings of grief due to the death or loss of a loved one.

Mystical travelers can live their lives singularly, but they'll always gravitate toward other advanced souls. If you get a group of mystical travelers together, there's almost nothing they can't do. While they can't change life charts, they *can* minimize them. Since they're part of Azna's army, they can create miracles and interfere, just as She can.

## Q: Do mystical travelers rest between assignments on the Other Side, or do they just work all the time?

A: Mystical travelers absolutely do rest because they have a lot of spiritual knowledge to impart (but never in a pushy, converting way). In the process of doing this for Earth and other planets, they attain more spirituality for themselves, even as they glorify Jesus and our Creators.

No matter how bad you think this planet is, as Sylvia says, there's definitely a movement that more and more people are coming to the light and the realization that they're masters of their own souls, as Christ taught. And most advanced entities won't even come back to this world, but will instead go to others.

### Insight from My Spirit Guide

In 1991, Francine presented an extensive trance session on the mystical traveler. If some of this seems repetitive, you'll also see that she's trying to impart the full meaning of what it entails to those who want to become advanced souls. There's a lot of information here, but as my guide says, there can never be too much, because choosing to take on the mantle is probably the most important decision you'll ever make in any lifetime.

As there are only about 90 to 100 years left for this planet's human life, Francine says that the need for mystical travelers is especially critical now because we need more warriors than ever to fight the darkness. The evil in this battle is insidious—it doesn't just attack with guns or mortar shells, but with bigotry, prejudice, greed, and intolerance. Advanced souls defend against it all, in an attempt to show, as Jesus did, that the kingdom of God is not of this world.

In the fight against evil, mystical travelers cannot help but attract to them those who are truly righteous and seeking spiritual enlightenment because of their teachings and actions. (My other spirit guide, Raheim, says that some people will not only notice that there is a different light around these advanced souls, but will even go so far as to remark about it.) Some mystical travelers might become leaders, but that's not really what they're striving for; rather, their foremost goal is to get out the truth to the masses. A true mystical traveler will always try to bring enlightenment and the truth about God and the Other Side to all, while also instilling the fact that life on Earth is transitory and not the true reality of our existence.

Getting back to that trance with Francine, here it is:

> In the beginning of becoming a mystical traveler, you may have strange pains. This doesn't mean that you can put every twinge you experience on becoming a mystical traveler and not see a doctor, but you can also have adjustments made to your body and mind from the Other Side. Guides or spirit doctors can take out or adjust things that need to be taken care of—bloodless surgery is an example, but you must give permission, as no one here on my side can invade your body, soul, or mind without your specific consent. Thought processes, on the other hand, will be crystal clear, and things that used to bother you will dissipate.
>
> At first, until you get into the habit or groove, you will have to monitor your words. Judgment of others is not allowed— although you can condemn those who *do* judge, along with

their wrongdoings or cruel acts. It's better to be quiet if you're saying something hurtful (or what you call "catty") to make yourself appear more important. It seems that this world thrives on negative press, and not only about celebrities. People judge everyone for no reason . . . other than their own often-misguided opinions.

Mystical travelers can emit any of the Rays of light; if they don't pick one then they emit the royal blue Ray. They also have their "third eye" opened, which can cause headaches for a while—it's not a migraine, but like a pressure in the forehead or a tight band around the head.

You could even feel your third eye pulsate, which means that information is coming in—and unlike Sylvia, you can even help yourself. She's never been able to . . . what she gets seems to just go right through her, without first stopping to give her information about herself. I don't mean that she's completely blind when it comes to herself, but she didn't take on her abilities to use them in a selfish way. Of course she's not more holy or advanced than others; I think her psychic ability is merely a tube that always goes outward.

Don't be concerned if what first comes through your third eye is negative because, as we know, this is a negative planet. But if you get negative thoughts unlike before, rather than just ignoring them, begin to ask where they're coming from and what you can do to nullify or work to solve them. No matter what the specific problem is, if you evoke Mother God you may be surprised that you're given a loophole or solution, even if it means you must go through it to get to the Other Side and make it better.

⸸

Mystical travelers have the power to create their own harmonic conversion, and when many of them get together, they can practically move mountains of negativity, either personally or on a worldwide scale. By coming together, miracles are common, and hordes of angels are at their disposal. Mystical travelers have all phyla of angels around them, from the Seraphim and Cherubim to the Archangels, the Powers, and the Thrones and

Municipalities (which are the armies of our Mother and Father, respectively). They also have powerful guides as well as passed-over loved ones who help when necessary.

Mystical travelers have the ability to look right into the Akashic Records, which are the complete records of everything in creation, and which are constantly changing and ongoing. At first what they see can be random, but over time advanced souls learn to control it to be more specific for a particular person, place, or thing. They can also freely come and go to the Other Side without any depletion of energy, visiting all of our Home's halls and temples, which are made with beautiful marble and are marvelous to behold.

[See *Temples on the Other Side* for more information.]

Mystical travelers go to the Council and then to the Hall of Wisdom to acquire knowledge or orders, or to find out how to bring about better conclusions to difficult situations. When they go into the Temple of Mystical Travelers and Mission-life Entities, their advanced status causes a beam of light to come down upon them, followed by a gleaming crystal. They're then allowed to ask for directions about a certain problem they might be having, and the voice from the crystal speaks. Often, they'll see a vision of Jesus, Azna, or the Father God . . . most of the time the reciprocation is with Azna.

Mystical travelers will eventually gain information on all their past lives and will have memory of speaking with God, especially our Mother. Their appearance on the Other Side will be that of a 30-year-old, like most entities, so they don't take on a visage of an older and wiser person as some members of the Council do.

When these advanced souls die, they immediately go Home. (Now, no entities ever suffer—no matter what you see, they're already gone even though you might think that they're suffering.) If they go on to other planets, they appear at the age of 30 as well; they stay there for as long as needed, and then they exit out. This might make some of you feel that mystical travelers are aliens who came from another world in a UFO, but entities on other planets are actually very advanced. They seem to recognize the avatars who have come to teach and help them. In fact, there is no need to incarnate and grow to adulthood on other worlds—mystical travelers can just appear and be recognized, and when their work is completed, they can simply leave.

As you become a more advanced mystical traveler, you'll find that the good things you like about yourself are enhanced and any undesirable traits seem to fade. This becomes especially apparent when you go back to the Other Side after living your final life on Earth, for it is then that you *truly* become a mystical traveler and go through a beautiful ceremony that seals the mantle you've taken on. Remember that you can back out before the final ceremony with no guilt, and still use the tools you've been given . . . although they won't carry the real power that they would have otherwise.

This ceremony entails repeating your oath to be a mystical traveler and is done in the presence of Azna, the Mother God. Here you'll not only receive a soul-binding mental mantle, but you'll also be bestowed a physical one in the form of what you might refer to as a capelike garment. The physical mantle is woven in silver, gold, and purple; it is extremely strong and made out of some type of gossamer material. While it looks very much like a cobweb, nothing negative can penetrate it.

This garment has a hood that can cover your head—the hood also has a point that can come over the top, which can be pulled down to reach your chest. The mantle is fully draped all the way around, and even your hands will be covered by points of this woven fabric. It has great, huge sunbursts of gold through it, and the whole of it looks iridescent. You use this garment when you travel and visit other planets, but you don't usually wear it on the Other Side.

**Sylvia:** I hope you've found this information from Francine to be helpful, especially as you begin the process of becoming a mystical traveler.

# CHAPTER ELEVEN

# SPECIAL RITUALS AND THE PREPARATION PROCESS

Everyone will take on the mantle of the mystical traveler in different ways. Even though you do God's bidding, it's your free-will choice to go as far as you want with it, and no one judges you, especially not our Creators. Maybe you're afraid that you're not worthy or that you'll rebel against the whole mystical-traveler vocation—even if that's true, it won't matter, since either way you'll still find yourself better off and more spiritual.

I can't say this enough: *Whether you realize it or not, God's will and your own are the same, and it's always been that way.* You're just giving full recognition to it now. Also, don't forget that you left this as an option on the Other Side, so becoming a mystical traveler isn't something that's forced upon you without your consent. If you make it through the induction ceremony in the next chapter and still feel that you're going to rebel, or even if you don't want to do the ceremony at all, nothing negative will happen to you. You will have been given extra tools for protection, no matter what.

If you're certain that you'd like to become a mystical traveler, you should begin to prepare yourself, which is what the following information is all about.

*Special Rituals for the Mystical Traveler*

Before we get to the preparation process to become a truly advanced soul, I'd like to mention the importance of rituals for such a soul. When I was writing my book *Secret Societies . . . and How They Affect Our Lives Today,* I didn't agree with some of the strange and bizarre rites I came across, but if they please other people and aren't ruled by secrecy and the occult, then I defend others' right to any kind of observance they want. It is only when folks begin to hurt themselves and encompass themselves and others with fear that I do rebel.

The rituals of the mystical traveler aren't worrisome in any way. And while it's not necessary to follow these practices religiously, they will really help you:

— **First**, while I've already mentioned how powerful prayer and affirmations can be, I'd like to stress how important it is that you surround yourself with multiple lights when you do them. Green is for health; gold is for higher and infused knowledge; purple is for high spirituality; and, of course, the white light of the Holy Spirit is held closest to the body. Also ask for the Eight Golden Keys to become stronger within you and to keep filling your soul with their power and protection.

— **Next**, I'd like to talk about the importance of numbers. Everyone resonates to a different numeral; for the mystical traveler, it happens to be 9. (It's interesting to note that that's Azna's number as well.) You can add up the letters in your name—mine, for instance, is Sylvia (6) Browne (6) and adds up to 12, which reduces down to 3 (1 + 2). A 3 is a trinity number, which pays special homage to our Mother, our Father, and Jesus Christ. The number 6 is considered a double trinity, while 9 is a triple trinity . . . which is why it's so important to advanced souls. (However, please don't worry if your personal number isn't 3, 6, or 9—no numeral is better or worse than any other, and it's all about what feels best for you.)

Mystical travelers tend to prefer asking
and good fortune for themselves and oth
you go to my lectures, you'll notice that 1
start my meditations at 9 P.M. When I hold
the afternoons, I'll start the meditation at 3, :
trinity numbers. Yet although the Catholic (
"novenas," I find it funny that no one can ar.
ask why 9 days are so important to them or v
angels' hour—that is, when everyone stops fo.
say a small prayer when a church bell chimes at

— **Finally,** it's great and wondrous if you can
cal travelers to program with you at the same ti
will happen. (Yes, I did say "miracles"—rememb
God is the miracle worker.) This practice creates a gi.
that brings people to you, which is why my church
of e-mails and letters about healings that have happ
as problems concerning money, marriage, children,
that have been solved. We have so many mystical trav
prayer or crisis line who pray together every night at
those put on our list that miracles are bound to happen.

Even if you're not attached to a group, do use th
Light a white candle at 9 o'clock and say or ask for what y
If I'm out at 9 A.M. or 9 P.M., I mentally do this . . . so if y
always get somewhere to do your rituals at the specific time
do them in your mind. At first you'll probably forget, but a
goes on, it will automatically become a part of you.

Francine says that even though you're a direct emissary
God, you'll find that on the whole your life gets easier when
perform these rituals. They aren't meant to interfere with y
life lessons, but they can help you conquer adversity more eas.
When the soul is in sync with God, it does smooth a lot of t
edge of heartache, pain, and grief.

The F

N
Pleas
no m
help
here

and

o
o
t

## *Four-Week Preparation Process*

Now it's time to prepare yourself to become a mystical traveler. Please note that it's vital that you meditate during the process, but no meditation should ever take the place of seeing a physician for help with a medical problem. The meditations I'll share with you here are the ones Francine gave me when I was going through this. Getting ready to be a mystical traveler takes about four weeks, and the procedure is as follows:

### 1. The Passive Week

During this first week, the "warrior in you" begins to come out. You may feel tense and want to be left alone, and old feelings of hurt and rejection will definitely come up. You'll feel short-tempered, to the point that the slightest thing can set you off: A simple phrase that you'd normally just slough off can easily get blown out of proportion. You question your life and what you have done, along with what you *should* have done. It's almost like you don't feel right in your own skin, or as the old saying goes, you feel "beside yourself."

Doubts filter in, to the point that you may want to give up, perhaps causing you to feel *This is all foolish, and who needs it? Isn't life hard enough without taking on more? I'm going to get to the Other Side anyway, and after all these lives, I'm already very tired.* You'll find yourself going through many variations on these themes, and you could fall into the "poor me" syndrome of *No one appreciates me— does God even love me?* Then you get mad at yourself for doubting.

As you can see, this first week is a mess . . . so why on earth is it called "passive"? It's because although the warrior part of you is making itself known, *you* must stay passive—as hard as it is, you cannot act on these feelings of depression. Your soul knows that you're getting ready to embark upon this huge change, and the flesh doesn't like change. So you could say that the "earthbound you" is fighting the "spiritual you."

When I went through the first week of the process, I felt as if I were in labor. Yes, I wanted the baby—but, damn, I certainly didn't want hours upon hours of nonstop pain. The only thing I can tell you is that it helps if you get a hobby or even pretend that you have one. I also took lots of rest periods and more or less stayed away from people. I didn't do any readings that week, which shocked everyone because even when I'm sick, my ability still works. I may have seemed quiet and passive to those around me, but there was a storm raging inside, and I was afraid I'd bite someone's head off. Even though it was more than 20 years ago, I still remember it like it was yesterday . . . I never doubted God, but I did doubt me.

You'll have plenty of time to be a social warrior later, so be reclusive during this first week and go on walks and rides by yourself. Don't consume any sugar, eat blandly, and drink lots of water—at least eight glasses a day to cleanse your system. Try to rest as much as you can, even if you have a family and a job. I know it's not easy, but it's so important that you do so during these first seven days.

✟

The first week's meditation is what we call "the Obelisk meditation":

> Sit or lie in a prone position. Relax every part of your body, starting at your feet. Pull the Rays of color through your feet, ankles, calves, thighs, and buttocks; and then move them through the trunk of your body. Breathe deeply and slowly—most of us breathe too shallowly, so hold your hands on your diaphragm to see if you are in fact breathing deeply.
>
> Move the Rays up your back and into each organ . . . bring them through your neck and down your shoulders, upper arms, lower arms, wrists, and fingers. Come back up your neck and into your face; around your mouth, nose, eyes, and ears; and to

*the top of your head. Ask that all your chakras be open yet protected by the Rays. Then go behind your eyes into your physical brain and then into your soul, thus balancing the intellect and emotion.*

*As you lie or sit here quietly, you begin to see a small grassy knoll. In the middle of the knoll is a beautiful marble fountain that has a large rim around it that you can sit on. You do so, relaxing there in the peaceful solitude and enjoying the sound of the rippling water.*

*In the middle of the fountain is a beautiful pink and opalescent marble obelisk. This obelisk symbolizes the finger of God pointing upward, as well as a symbol of your ascension to a higher level and your commitment to God. As you look at the obelisk, you see a vision of the Mother God in full regalia, carrying Her golden sword and wearing Her golden breastplate. As She extends Her sword, you feel it touch your heart and soul, and all the bitterness and angst you have felt in the last week just subsides.*

*While the vision of Azna fades away, start bringing yourself up to full and complete consciousness so that you come out of your meditation refreshed and relaxed.*

## 2. The Week of Sweetness

The second week of the process may lull you into a false sense of security. I felt like this at first, but the more I pondered it, the more I realized that I was just being given a break for what was to come.

Here you forget the toughness of last week—again, as with childbirth, the pain and doubts and bitterness are gone. Your spirits are high, and you feel that you've taken a giant step at this point. You're not aware of what lies ahead in the next three weeks, but you know that nothing this important could ever be easy.

If something comes too easily, I've never trusted it anyway. The old saying "If it's too good to be true" usually ends up being all too accurate, as very little in life is gained without hard work and sweat. Even people who win the lottery oftentimes go bankrupt or end up worse off than they were before.

Many avatars or holy men and women go through terrible tortures to purify themselves, such as staying in a desert, fasting for long periods, or beating themselves. Preparing to become a mystical traveler is nothing like that; it's more in the mind and soul that you're tested. Yes, it can be rough, but it's nothing you can't stand. You're always keeping your eye on the golden ring and the benefits you will attain.

In fact, this is the week where you'll feel like you do when you're in love. I call it "the week of raging endorphins," as nothing will bother you. Someone could be sarcastic or mean, and you'll just float through it. You're on an incredible natural high, which nothing or no one will be able to shake. No matter what comes along, you'll have such a degree of optimism that you'll absolutely know every outcome will have a happy ending. This may seem extreme, but I bet you could even get in a wreck or watch your house burn down, and you'd simply shrug and say, "Well, they're only things, which are replaceable."

This is probably the closest you could ever come on Earth to experiencing how we feel on the Other Side. I liken it to when I was so infatuated with my first love that the world seemed to hold nothing but joy and music. I was so thrilled just to see him . . . and I was even thrilled when I didn't see him, for then I could think about him. I hardly ate or slept, but it didn't matter because I was so in love. I got that horrible Asian flu and coughed so hard that I broke three ribs, but I didn't really notice that much thanks to my all-encompassing feelings.

The second week feels just like this—it's saturated with sweetness and light, love and total optimism. I've never taken drugs, but I don't know what drug could possibly compare with this sensation of knowing that you could conquer the world. Of course it can't last, not on this plane, but I often think that if the Other Side is half as good as the way I felt this second week, then *heaven* is indeed the right word for it.

The meditation that follows this second week is also beautiful:

*Again, you sit straight up in a comfortable position or lie prone. But this time, concentrate on one of the Rays' colors that fits your mood. Whether it is orange, mauve, gold, or green, again thread it through your body. Whereas you wanted that cranky bitterness of the first week to be released and go away forever, you want to keep as much of the feelings of this week as possible. So ask that a great amount of that euphoric residue you have felt in the second week be left behind.*

*You find yourself in a field again, surrounded by tall trees and beautiful mountains in the distance. You listen to the sounds of birds and notice that the flowers are the sweetest you have ever smelled, but they are not overpowering. You look above you and see the Seraphim and Cherubim, and then you hear the most heavenly singing you have ever heard. You are not even aware of the words, as the tonal quality is unearthly in its beauty. You never want it to end. It is like a moment cut out of the fabric of time that is beyond description. Even the colors of the grass, the sky, the birds, and the sun seem to breathe life. There is no hue on this side that lives and vibrates like this.*

*You sit there in this serenity and contemplate your life. All the things you were so worried about do not seem to be a part of you anymore . . . it is like it was someone else's life, or a dream that was meaningless and forgotten. You can take this all in for a time, but reality will have its way. So you will gradually come back to yourself, retaining the full memory of the sounds and the feelings of love and serenity you have experienced.*

### 3. The Week of Confusion

The third week truly is confusing. As great as the last week was, this one is *disruptive* in all senses of the word. You're not angry, but it does seem that life has become a puzzle, and you don't know where the pieces are—and even if you *could* locate them, you wouldn't know how to fit them together.

You'd almost swear that you'd been struck with senility, as things that used to make sense don't anymore. Unlike the first week, where you felt almost robotic because you didn't want to inflict your mood on anyone, it now seems as if you're swimming through mud. You can still make it through your days, but your energy is so low that the smallest tasks seem almost insurmountable: I remember that just the very thought of getting up, dressing, and fixing my hair seemed as difficult as climbing Mount Everest. You cry if you can't find your car keys; even a telephone call from a salesperson can set you off. Thanks to the energy drain and the feeling of futility—that is, wondering what in the hell is the use or purpose of all this—you really feel like giving up.

Thank God it only lasts for a week since it's as if you don't have a sense of yourself, of what you're doing, or even of what you're *going* to do with yourself. Although you might genuinely think that you're ready for the funny farm, don't call the doctor just yet. You're merely experiencing malaise (and really, pardon the expression, not giving a damn), which couldn't be more different from what you felt in the second week. Just as you wished that one would never end, this week drags to the point that you think you're always going to feel this way.

Your intellect does rise up during these times, which you tell yourself is due to your training, but that good old emotion gets in there and says, "Yeah, so what? I feel lousy now, and I want it to stop." Fortunately, the bad parts don't last forever in life . . . but *un*fortunately, neither does the heavenly euphoria. Your soul simply can't support any of these emotions or feelings for more than seven days.

It's good during this week to consume light proteins such as chicken, fish, turkey, and eggs, which you can put on salads. Also, drink plenty of fruit juices and water, and eat lots of very green vegetables. Stay away from anything greasy, oily, or rich because you're still trying to build up your immune system as well as purify it. As this third week comes to an end, your energy will get really high. It's like after you've had a flu or cold and then the day comes when you're over it and you feel like yourself again . . . but in this case, you'll be even better than your old self.

Be aware that no one else in your life is going to understand what you're going through—they may think that you're in a mood, that something is on your mind, or that you just don't feel good. So it can really help if you make contact with someone else who's also in training. For example, when I went through this process many years ago, I was part of a group, so at least the other members and I could communicate with each other and feel better because we knew that others were going through the same thing.

Many individuals have gone through this process but didn't realize what it was—people don't always know when they're being prepared to be mystical travelers and ultimately give up their will to God. While nuns and priests had the right idea to present themselves unconditionally to Jesus (or in the case of nuns, to be married to him), they didn't need to take the vows of charity, celibacy, and obedience.

You don't have to live an austere life, but do make sure that your soul isn't poor from lack of giving. Yes, you can give your money, but how about your time, energy, love, and hope? As someone once said, hope is a bird that resides in the soul and never quits singing. (Please note that there isn't a special meditation for this week—but do feel free to use one of your own choosing if you feel you need it.)

### 4. The Week of Belligerence

The fourth week is the one you have to be most diligent about, as it could *also* be referred to as "the week of temptation." You have to watch your false ego, being careful that you don't feel you're the only one who has the real truth, and that everyone else is wrong or misled.

Naturally, there are those who are more advanced mystical travelers, but you can't be ego bound and feel that you're better than anyone else. You may get into the mind-set that you're more advanced or on a higher level than others are, so you'll want to fight against any person, religion, or belief that doesn't go along with you or even tries to understand what you're doing or why you're doing it. You feel like getting on a soapbox—or even worse, you try to convert others to your belief with a hard sell.

But what if you just want everyone to feel and know what you do? Well, you can in time be a teacher for those who desire to become mystical travelers and even hold classes, but you can *never* force your beliefs on people. The teachings of an advanced soul are for information and not conversion.

You must remember that taking on the mantle is your own private covenant with Mother and Father God, and it's not your duty to call others. Our Parents will direct those souls Themselves, or the individuals will do their own seeking until they find what they're looking for. Much like individuals are called upon to become rabbis, imams, ministers, priests, nuns, or monks, so can souls rise up to become mystical travelers. Yet they must search, pray, and give their will to God all on their own.

✠

The meditation for the fourth and final week goes like this:

*Again, sit comfortably or lie in a prone position. You will be using silver light this time, which is one of the colors of the mantle. But first, thread purple and then gold individually through your whole body, starting at your toes and going through your feet, ankles, calves, thighs, buttocks, and back. Make sure that you go through all your organs, from the reproductive, lymphatic, and neurological systems to the intestinal tract: the appendix, stomach, gallbladder, pancreas, heart, lungs, and so on. Ask that your skeletal structure and all your tendons, muscles, and ligaments become stronger; and ask that blood goes to all the places in your body that need more circulation.*

Next, take each color up through your neck, both back and front; and then into the thyroid gland, mouth, ears, nose, and eyes; and into the pineal, pituitary, and hypothalamus glands. Ask that your skin texture be better and that all systems, be they named or unnamed, begin to function better than they ever have. This is both for chronic ills and prevention.

Take yourself to a meadow, along with your Eight Keys and Seven Rays. While you do not have your mantle yet, you are still ahead of the game of life with these extra tools. Ask that your angels, guide, passed-over loved ones from all your lives, Azna, God the Father, Jesus, and any and all of the messiahs come to attend you.

This meadow you are in is full of golden daffodils, and mountains are in the distance. You suddenly notice that a silver tube is descending on top of you, and it goes right through your body—from the top of your head to the tips of your toes. You can now be a planter of light columns who gives honor to God. Say, "Every time I step, I will plant a light column of love, peace, and spiritual awareness. Wherever I walk now, I say that each time I put my feet down, I want a light column to be planted, be it at work, at lectures, on planes, at parties, or wherever I walk."

Focus on the beautiful meadow that is filled with golden daffodils . . . they sparkle like bright burnished gold in the sunlight. In the distance you can see a purple mountain, and you notice that a light breeze has come up that gently blows across your face and body. Everything is so serene.

All of a sudden, large and ugly brown blocks begin to appear in front of you, obstructing your view. Each block may say "poor self-esteem," "isolation," "depression," "phobias," "fears," "worries," "family problems," "financial concerns," "marriage troubles," or "past memories that haunt you." "I should have done" and "I wish I had not done" are also labeled on these blocks, which keep piling higher and higher.

Yet you are now aware that you can reach inside and pull some of your silver column out, and it goes right back into its *original shape. It is malleable in your hands—you form it into a ball and then throw it at these blocks, which are your own individual problems. At first nothing happens, as these are things that have been with you for years, even from past lives. In many ways, especially negative ones, they have become part of you and even victimized you.*

*You pull another part of the silver column out and throw it at the blocks. Again and again you do this. After many throws at the blocks with great energy, you hear a crack. Another ball of silver light causes a loud noise, and the blocks come crashing down. You walk over and are so surprised at how big and ominous these blocks were. You will be stunned by how heavy these problems were that you have carried. No wonder you felt so tired and depressed at times. Right before your eyes, they become reduced to little brown wispy shards, and a breeze comes to blow them away. Then the golden daffodils perk up . . . and you, like the phoenix, rise out of the ashes fresh and new and ready to face the world, free from all the heavy and needless blocks of life.*

*As you come back to yourself, you do not feel out of sorts, overly euphoric, confused, belligerent, deficient, or tired. You feel like yourself, only better—a cleansed self without all the impediments that you have dealt with for all these years. The problems and things represented by the ugly brown blocks now seem like far-off memories, almost like a dream not fully remembered. They do not have any aftermath; this does not mean that you will never again have a worry, but all of the old behavioral overlays are indeed gone.*

And now, without further ado, it's time to accept the mantle of the mystical traveler. Just turn the page. . . .

✢ ✢ ✢

# Chapter Twelve

# THE INDUCTION
# CEREMONY

Now that you're finally ready to take on the mystical traveler's mantle, it's time to focus on your induction ceremony. You should choose a date that is significant for you—while you may immediately think of your birthday, it can be any day that you choose. Catholicism celebrates "feast days," so you might want to see this as your own special feast day. But whatever you call it, it's a great and glorious day.

Setting a date for the ceremony helps you prepare; it's like sending out invitations for one of the most holy, memorable, and special occasions that you could ever experience. Of course everyone on the Other Side will already be aware of when you're going to take your sacred oath, but like a birthday or an anniversary party, it's more for you than for others. When you have the ceremony to become a mystical traveler, everyone at Home who's been with you in this or any other life attends, along with the Council, your guide and angels, Jesus, and Mother and Father God.

Before your big day, it's natural to experience some nervousness and feelings of excitement, much like before a wedding. I even feel this way before a lecture or going on Montel's show . . . because I want to do the best I can, the fear is always there. When I was much younger, I tended to look around for an exit sign right before I'd go onstage, in case I just couldn't do it. Of course I never bolted, but it was often a comforting thought.

I remember the first pay-per-view special I ever did. Montel and Hay House had put a lot of capital into it, and the thought of failing them or causing them to lose money was more than I could bear. Since I knew what was riding on me, I obsessed about it for a good month. When the night finally came, I thought my heart would either stop or come through my mouth. Right before I made my entrance, my husband at the time came over and whispered, "Dead woman walking." Although that's actually how I felt, it made me laugh and took the edge off. But thank God no one lost any money on their investment.

That might be akin to how you'll be feeling—while the ceremony isn't like a performance, being on a stage is a good analogy. I think the permanency of the mantle (that is, that it lasts forever) can be elating but scary. The fear you experience usually comes down to not wanting to let God or others down.

Before we go any further, please remember that you don't have to join a church or even be a minister for this, as it's your own private ceremony. Yet if you think that you won't be administering to people, you're wrong. The very act of becoming a mystical traveler will set you into motion—you'll either be pushed toward others, or they'll be pulled toward you because your light beams forth at them.

☦

During the ceremony, it's helpful to light a candle, particularly any color that corresponds with the Seven Rays of God. (Don't use red or black candles, as red is angry and black signals darkness.) Try to do your ceremony on the third hour: 12, 3, 6, or 9. Nine o'clock is the best time if you can do it because, as you know, Azna resonates to that number, which is a triple trinity.

Now, let's say that you can't get to a candle for some reason—well, just light it in your mind and reaffirm the Eight Golden Keys and Seven Rays. Take a few minutes to go over them mentally or aloud, and visualize the colors of the Rays. Even if you simply go through them by name, this helps to ingrain them in your soul. I know that most of you who wish to become mystical travelers will prepare yourselves and set aside enough time to do all of this properly, but in the worst-case scenario, all you have to do is quickly reaffirm the Keys and Rays. Saving time can also come in handy if you're suddenly thrust into a negative situation.

Francine has shared the ceremony to become a mystical traveler, which she states you can do alone or in a group. If you've decided that it's not for you, stop here and just take what you've learned with you. True, you won't be able to effectively use the Rays like mystical travelers can, but everyone should live by the Eight Golden Keys. Advanced souls just do so every day, so they carry a greater power in healing, neutralizing negativity, and ascending their souls by giving up their will. Once again, please don't feel that you could ever be less in God's eyes—it's your decision to advance your soul *for you*. The mystical-traveler vocation is truly not for everyone.

With that being said, here is the ceremony for taking on the mantle, in Francine's own words (which you may want to speak into a tape recorder first, and then play when you're ready):

*I would like for you to stand, but any of you who don't want to do so may sit. Just let your arms be at your sides, and relax your body. As I'm speaking, you may begin to notice that you feel a light fluttering around you. That's because the angels are congregating around you, along with your guides, your passed-over loved ones, other mystical travelers, the Council, Jesus, and Mother and Father God.*

*See yourself in a meadow that stretches for miles. There are no obstructions, except for high golden mountains in the background, which look as they do at sunset or sunrise. On these mountains stand all the phyla of angels: The Cherubim and*

*Seraphim are singing softly; the Archangels, Virtues, Powers, Carrions, Dominions, Thrones, Principalities, and uncounted throngs of "regular" angels are all watching.*

*You begin to notice that where you stand is strewn with rose petals, and the smell is heady. You walk a little way and become aware of a rose arbor—behind it, there is a garden filled with every flower imaginable. You hear the most beautiful songs of birds in the distance; feel the warm sun on your face; and enjoy a light, fragrant breeze that dances around you. You're at such peace, and you have the sensation of familiarity and of being home.*

*Azna, the Mother God, and Her angel army of Thrones begin to march down the mountain, and they're all dressed in gold. Behind them are the Archangels, who are clad in purple, and the Principalities, who wear emerald green. God the Father stands a short distance in front of you, and our Lord stands to the left of you. The Council, loved ones, and guides are a little to the right of you, looking on, pleased and smiling. Our Mother comes with Her arms above Her head: In Her right hand, She carries a golden sword; in Her left hand, She carries a golden scepter. Very quickly, She places Herself behind but above you.*

*There is a golden mantle with iridescent lights that reflect purple, green, white, orange, and blue, almost like a rainbow . . . but gold is the predominant color. It's poised above your head, and you speak these words, which go out into the universe: "Dear Mother, dear Father, I embrace this mantle. From all my lifetimes and all that I've seen and experienced, I now walk totally with Thee. This is the culmination of all my lives, and I have come full circle to embrace my spirituality." It seems that time stops now. The entire universe is quiet because the Other Side is listening and watching. Only the slight fluttering of wings is discernible.*

*"Dear Holy Spirit, which is the love between the Mother and Father God," you continue, "I ask now that my will is cemented with that of the Mother, the Father, and the Son . . . that from this moment on, I will be in the Legion of Merit, Service, and*

Spirituality that is only between myself and you. I wish to be in the army of the mystical traveler and do your bidding."

With Her arms extended and a beautiful smile on Her face, Azna is now standing in front of you with Her sword upheld. She puts Her sword in front of you and then places it on both of your shoulders, as if you're being knighted. Gradually the mantle begins to drop, and you don't feel drained, but rather that glorious light is going through your entire body. You know, as you never have before, that you are completely steeped in overwhelming love.

Your senses are enhanced more than ever: You seem to hear everything, including the sounds of angels, and it's almost like you can feel the flowers grow. Your eyes can make out every detail, and you inhale all the floral scents. Your heart and soul are opened to the Mother; your intellect is opened to the Father and the Son. Your whole body seems to vibrate with an unconditional love that you've never been aware of before.

Now the mantle finishes dropping, which you feel as just a small pressure. You may think that the mantle would be heavier, but it's light and becomes part of your soul. You barely feel it on your skin, and then it goes deep inside. It immediately cements in your soul, mind, and body, including every organ. It closes softly around you, and you feel as if you're being encompassed and hugged by love. The mantle is now branded upon you by your will, and it is forever. No matter how far you go—even to the ends of any universe or to the ends of time—it will always be with you.

You declare, "By my will, I have received this mantle that is a symbol of my devotion. My will is Thy will, and Thy will be done."

Feel the power. See our Mother strike the pose of the ultimate Warrior Queen Who fights negativity, but also see Her as the ultimate in love and benevolence. See our Lord embracing you with all his love and acceptance. Feel the breath of the Father God on your face as He advances, strong, regal, and magnificent. You feel the full essence of this mighty Creator, *and you sense His strength and unconditional love. The inner healing of your soul begins as sparks of silver are sent through your entire body.*

*You finally say, "Dear God, hold these hands of the mystical traveler that can now heal. Soothe my tongue to speak truth, and use it to impart Your infused words through the eons that can hear beyond words that are spoken. Let my eyes see more than they have ever seen before, and let my third eye be fully open so that I can pierce through negative darkness. I will go wherever I am needed in the name of the Father, Mother, Holy Spirit, and our Lord Jesus Christ. In my right hand I will receive a golden sword to fight evil, and I will clamp my sword to my heart. I have the mantle that protects me; my mind and soul, which are branded with the love of Father and Mother; and my oath."*

*Feel the peace. Feel the magnificence of your soul rising up . . . stretching your soul so wide and knowing in your very being that you've answered the call, and Thy will has truly been done. Stand for a few moments basking in this sacred moment, not humble but proud in your true "I am."*

*Azna now walks behind you and makes it known to all that you have joined Her army. You feel that you are absolutely part of the ranks of those who have gone before you, and will come after you, to win the battle against darkness.*

Now that you've completed the entire process of becoming a mystical traveler, it's up to you as to how you proceed. But even if you just take care of those around you, that's enough; after all, this is something that's between you and God.

Once you've gone through the ceremony, you'll begin to see changes. They may be small ones at first, but they'll get stronger and bigger as you use your Keys and Rays. As the old worry, guilt, and even pain disappear, the joy you feel will be indescribable. And with all this knowledge that you have garnered, I don't want you to quit learning, exploring, reading, and researching. No matter what texts you have read, especially those of a theological nature, you'll come to the understanding that white-souled enti-ties are researching and reaching up for knowledge to give love and adoration to our Creators.

This brings to mind something I wrote many years ago:

*"Where are you going?" said my soul in a quiet corner all alone.*

*"I'm going where I please," said my willful heart. "I have passions to experience and life in abundance to live."*

*"Where are you going?" silently breathed my soul.*

*"I am intellect," said my mind. "I can rationalize every-thing. I have mind power to learn and mouths to listen to and books to read."*

*"Where are you going?" again whispered my soul.*

*"I have music to enjoy and people to love and sunsets to see," said my emotion.*

*"Do you know where you are going?" my soul again replied.*

*"I am the body," was the answer. "I am full of organs, muscle, and bone; and I must excel in life."*

*"But," said the soul ever so softly, "I am that which breathes with God . . . all of these are nothing until you bring them into harmony with me."*

I know that for your entire life, you're going to be proud that you're a mystical traveler. While there will still be times when things get tough, the healings and blessings you receive will out-weigh any negativity. Congratulations!

*God love you. I do.*
***Sylvia***

✝ ✝ ✝

# About the Author

**Sylvia Browne** is the #1 *New York Times* best-selling author and world-famous psychic medium who appears regularly on *The Montel Williams Show* and *Larry King Live,* as well as making countless other media and public appearances. With her down-to-earth personality and great sense of humor, Sylvia thrills audiences on her lecture tours and still has time to write numerous immensely popular books. She has a master's degree in English literature and plans to write as long as she can hold a pen.

Sylvia is the president of the Sylvia Browne Corporation; and is the founder of her church, the Society of Novus Spiritus, located in Campbell, California. Please contact her at: **www.sylvia.org,** or call **(408) 379-7070** for further information about her work. Sylvia is also featured on an additional Website: **www.SpiritNow.com**.

✝ ✝ ✝

# Hay House Titles of Related Interest

*YOU CAN HEAL YOUR LIFE, the movie,*
starring Louise L. Hay & Friends
(available as a 1-DVD program and an expanded 2-DVD set)
Watch the trailer at: **www.LouiseHayMovie.com**

☦

*THE ANSWER IS SIMPLE . . . Love Yourself, Live Your Spirit!*
by Sonia Choquette

*THE ASTONISHING POWER OF EMOTIONS: Let Your Feelings Be
Your Guide,* by Esther and Jerry Hicks (The Teachings of Abraham®)

*COURAGEOUS DREAMING: How Shamans Dream the World
into Being,* by Alberto Villoldo, Ph.D.

*IN MY OWN WORDS: An Introduction to My Teachings and
Philosophy,* by His Holiness The Dalai Lama; edited by Rajiv Mehrotra

*LED BY FAITH: Rising from the Ashes of the Rwandan Genocide,*
by Immaculée Ilibagiza, with Steve Erwin

*MESSAGES FROM SPIRIT: The Extraordinary Power of Oracles,
Omens, and Signs,* by Colette Baron-Reid

*THE POWER OF INTENTION: Learning to Co-create
Your World Your Way,* by Dr. Wayne W. Dyer

*THE SPONTANEOUS HEALING OF BELIEF: Shattering the Paradigm
of False Limits,* by Gregg Braden

*THE TIMES OF OUR LIVES: Extraordinary True Stories of Synchronicity,
Destiny, Meaning, and Purpose,* by Louise L. Hay & Friends

☦

All of the above are available at your local bookstore,
or may be ordered by contacting Hay House (see next page).

✣

We hope you enjoyed this Hay House book. If you'd like to receive
a free catalog featuring additional Hay House books and products, or
if you'd like information about the Hay Foundation, please contact:

Hay House, Inc.
P.O. Box 5100
Carlsbad, CA 92018-5100

**(760) 431-7695** or **(800) 654-5126**
**(760) 431-6948 (fax)** or **(800) 650-5115 (fax)**
**www.hayhouse.com®** • **www.hayfoundation.org**

✣

**Published and distributed in Australia by:** Hay House Australia Pty. Ltd.,
18/36 Ralph St., Alexandria NSW 2015 • *Phone:* 612-9669-4299
*Fax:* 612-9669-4144 • www.hayhouse.com.au

**Published and distributed in the United Kingdom by:** Hay House UK, Ltd.,
292B Kensal Rd., London W10 5BE • *Phone:* 44-20-8962-1230
*Fax:* 44-20-8962-1239 • www.hayhouse.co.uk

**Published and distributed in the Republic of South Africa by:** Hay House
SA (Pty), Ltd., P.O. Box 990, Witkoppen 2068 • *Phone/Fax:* 27-11-467-8904
orders@psdprom.co.za • www.hayhouse.co.za

**Published in India by:** Hay House Publishers India, Muskaan Complex,
Plot No. 3, B-2, Vasant Kunj, New Delhi 110 070 • *Phone:* 91-11-4176-1620
*Fax:* 91-11-4176-1630 • www.hayhouse.co.in

**Distributed in Canada by:** Raincoast, 9050 Shaughnessy St., Vancouver, B.C.
V6P 6E5 • *Phone:* (604) 323-7100 • *Fax:* (604) 323-2600 • www.raincoast.com

✣

Tune in to HayHouseRadio.com® for the best in inspirational
talk radio featuring top Hay House authors! And, sign up via the
Hay House USA Website to receive the Hay House online newsletter
and stay informed about what's going on with your favorite authors.
You'll receive bimonthly announcements about Discounts and Offers,
Special Events, Product Highlights, Free Excerpts, Giveaways, and more!
**www.hayhouse.com®**